If Hearts Had Training Wheels

a collection of poetry,

prose, thoughts, and art

by Ellen Everett

if hearts had training wheels

Front cover design, interior book design, artwork, and
illustrations created by Ellen Everett.

www.elleneverett.com

ISBN: 979-8-9858177-1-3

also by ellen everett

i saw you as a flower

acknowledgments

To my Mom and Dad; You are my favorite people in this world. Thank you for encouraging me from my roots to do what I love. From a young age, you have encouraged me to use the gifts God has given me and to share them with the world. Thank you for always believing in me, for supporting me, and for being incredible examples of a godly and pure love. Thank you for loving me and for bringing me years of wonderful memories and happiness. I am so thankful for our relationship. I have not always been easy; thank you for loving me as if I was. I love you.

To my siblings, Ben and Naomi; I feel so lucky to have grown up with you and do life with you. I wouldn't want to call anyone else my brother and sister. I'm so proud of both of you for the people you have become and am so thankful for each of you. Thank you for a lifetime of aggravating and loving each other.

To my Poppa and Nana; My heart aches writing this to you both. Poppa, I love you. It breaks my heart that I cannot pull into your gravel driveway again and see you working in your garden. You were a beautiful example of how to live. You always believed in me in all that I did. I can't wait to join you in heaven's gardens one day. Nana, you have always been an inspiration for my writing. You are such a gentle soul. If your memory was still with you, I know that you'd be so thrilled to read through these pages.

Thank you for years of walks through your flower gardens and for your pancake breakfasts. Thank you for introducing me to books and your love for reading. I love you endlessly. You are the best flower I know.

To the rest of my incredible family; Thank you for always supporting me, checking up on me, believing in me, and for reading my first book over and over. I am so grateful for your love and constant encouragement.

To Abby Green, my best friend; You came into my life and changed it instantly. You are a light to everyone you meet and inspire me daily. Thank you for being both the shoulder I cry on and for being the person that can always make me belly laugh. Thank you for always holding me accountable and for being the person I can always confide in. Thank you for never losing your excitement for life. I'm so grateful for our friendship.

To Douglas Dabbs, my first illustration professor; I cannot express in words how grateful I am for you. It is because of *you* that this project has been possible. You have a unique ability of helping students cultivate their skills and bring their ideas to life. You have been the catalyst for my growth as an artist, but you have given me a gift that extends far beyond the classroom. Your endless encouragement and support over the past few years has impacted my life forever. You have been a confidant, a role model, and a friend. Thank you for genuinely believing in me when I couldn't believe in myself.

To the rest of my MTSU art professors; and more specifically, Noel Lorson, Tony Rodriguez, Stefanie Cobb, and Sheri Selph, for continually encouraging me in my artistic endeavors. As well as being role models and inspirations, you have all equipped me with the skills and confidence I needed to make this project possible, and this is something I will carry with me and continue to develop for the rest of my life. I am forever grateful.

To the entire Oakdale community; my wonderful teachers, ball coaches, families and friends I have come to know and love; thank you for your immense support for *I Saw You As A Flower,* and simply in my entire up-bringing. I'm so thankful that my growing years were spent in this close-knit community. You have given a new meaning to community and have been a family to me. Thank you for encouraging me from a young age and continually supporting me in all that I do.

Above all, to the ultimate author, artist, and creator— my personal savior and redeemer— my Lord Jesus Christ.

And with all my love, to Kevin;

You've been the anchor in my stormy seas;
in waters calm, you've been my peace—
and I'll always keep a piece of you.

contents

CONTENTS

PART I
THE GRAVEL DRIVEWAY

PART II
THE SCENIC ROUTE

PART III
USING THE BRAKES

PART IV
THE UPHILL CLIMB

PART V

THE DOWNHILL COAST

A Note to My Readers

Dear Reader,

I have always had a hard time talking about my feelings. I tend to bottle things up and bury my emotions inside. Writing them down has been a way for me to process my life and heal. The paper is here for me in the way I would need a person to be. It is my venting ground. My place to unleash everything. I hope it is here for you in this way as well.

What you are about to read isn't just a result of me growing. This isn't just me developing my writing. This isn't just me mulling over words repeatedly in my mind until I have to spit them out. It is all of these things, yes. But more than that, this is me experiencing. It's me loving. It's me losing. It's me living. It's me dying. It's me sharing. I want you to know everything. I want you to heal. To feel. To find connection. I want you to know that you aren't alone. This isn't just a book I've written. These aren't just letterforms on paper. These aren't just words dressed up fancy.

This is my soul; so take it freely. Live in it for a moment. Fold over the corners of your favorite pages, write on me like graffiti. I want this book to be lived in. I want your art. I want your thoughts. This is my life and I want you to be a part of it; live in every room inside my heart. Make yourself comfortable. Light a candle, or two, or as many as you'd like. Stay for a while. I'm not just a story-teller. I'm living a story and I want you to live this story with me.

All my love,
Ellen

P.S.

Before you start reading this collection, I wanted to explain a few things that I think are important to know while reading these pages. When I write, I often go on long walks. I carry a notebook in hand and simply admire the world. I walk past flower fields and fences and neighborhoods. I stop by rivers and ponds and streams. I go to parking garages. I soak in the world around me. While I'm walking is usually when I quickly jot ideas down into my journal. Whatever comes to my mind, I scribble it down as quickly as possible so it doesn't run away from me. Most of the time, it is literally while my legs are still moving. So my journals are extremely messy. Anyways, I'm telling you this because I have included some scans of my original ideas for my poems throughout these pages. I'll have them placed next to the poems they coincide with. I've also sprinkled in a couple of notes people have written to me. I wanted this collection to be as raw and personal as possible; and I've realized I want to be more vulnerable and honest as a writer and a sharer of the human experience.

By including these scans of my journals, I wanted you to have a more intimate experience with these poems. I want you to see where they began and where they ended up. My writing never starts out perfect, and it never ends up perfect. It is a chaotic, personal, and messy process. Once the words walk around the page enough, they finally leave their footprints. They finally get to a point where I'm satisfied with them. I think this can be a testament to our lives. They won't ever be perfect; it's the journey that matters. The process. The little moments along the way. This is what makes living worthwhile. I hope this collection brings some light into your life and leaves its footprints on you as well.

If Hearts Had Training Wheels

PART I

THE GRAVEL DRIVEWAY

I first learned to ride a bike in my grandparents' long, gravel driveway. Fear swept over me as I climbed onto the bicycle without training wheels for the first time and it began teetering side to side. Thinking of falling could have kept me from riding it, but I wanted freedom more. I wanted to feel the wind in my hair and let it waltz against my cheeks and eyelashes. I wanted to feel alive. And I did feel alive. I was *especially* reminded of it when I crashed. And it happened many times. That gravel driveway absorbed it all; bloodied wrists, scraped knees, tread marks, and tear stains. I learned then that any time we begin something new, we will fail at it. We will have our share of falls regardless of how prepared we think we are.

My teenage years were similar to my time spent on the gravel driveway. Especially my first relationships. Crashing was inevitable—and like the gravel driveway, my heart was there absorbing every blow. I was young and enthusiastic, and filled with wonder; but I was naive. I have always been hopeful when it comes to people. Especially at this time in my life, I saw the best in everyone. I was seeing the world with tunnel vision; oblivious to any red flags in my peripheral. I overlooked everyone's flaws. I thought that because I wanted nothing except to share my heart with another person, that their intentions were the same.

I was wrong. I gave my heart to the wrong people; people who took advantage. It took me a while to realize that I hadn't been the one pedaling the bicycle at all. I was just an accessory in the basket. *Or maybe I wasn't even in the basket.* I had allowed one person in particular to control every aspect of my life. They thrived at my falls. Laughed at my scrapes. Caused many of them. I'd lost control of the bike without even realizing it.

This small section is about that period of my life. After this, I don't know if I'll ever write about it again. It has taken me a long time to recover and an even longer time to let go. Thankfully, I have found forgiveness.

My heart was left so battered and scuffed from this relationship, it is a wonder I was able to stand up on my own two feet again. Getting up off the ground came with a bitter taste on my tongue. Life felt unfair. I couldn't grasp why I was going through this situation when my intentions had always been pure. I so badly wished that my heart had training wheels, so I would have never known heartache or trauma. So I never would have fallen or lost control. When I finally let go of the bitterness, I was able to climb back onto the bicycle again. This time with more caution—and equipped with some scars as humble reminders.

Narrowing down my feelings and writing these poems has given me a closure and peace that has truly helped me to heal and move forward from this part of my life. I have ridden away from the gravel driveway and will never return again.

a b a n d o n m e n t

In the end of it all,
it is not you
who determines
the outcome of my life.
I choose whether or not
to allow my walls
to be riddled
by your overgrowth and ivy,
and my windows to collect
with your grime and mildew,
and my hinges to ripen with rust.
I am in charge of my own upkeeping,
so when the pipes leak
and the closets gather with clutter,
and the floorboards are left unswept
and begin to creak and groan,
I cannot blame you for this.

And although you may have
contributed to my decay,
I can choose
to wake up each morning
to dust the cobwebs,
and to unclog the gutters,
and to trim the hedges.

I will choose to
power-wash the siding,
and the porch,
and the concrete,
and I will watch your muck and fungus
run into the gravel driveway
and underneath the topsoil
to take root
into someone else's plot of earth.

where are the honeybees?

It must be winter forever;
I haven't seen the honeybees in a while
Even in the spring
they must be in hibernation
I have only encountered wasps and hornets
and yellow jackets and cicada killers
I have never had someone
who did anything but sting—
Where are the honeybees?
I need someone to pollinate me.
I have only been stripped, pillaged, plundered;
I have sacrificed and devoted and pledged myself
only to be vandalized, ransacked, crippled.
I have never wanted anything except
to be whole with someone—
not torn from and torn apart by—
Where are the honeybees?
I crave someone's sweetness;
someone who knows how to
congregate amongst the wildflowers.
Someone who generates new life.
Someone who will better me.

in places you aren't wanted

I have a splinter and I'm sure it must be you; who else
would be lodged underneath my skin without warning /
there was no sign of entry / you snuck inside me swiftly,
eager to find a passageway to my heart

the veins, you thought

the blood will pump through them

you were confident that you could make it / navigating
has always been your specialty / even if you had reached
my veins, my white blood cells are far too good at
detecting infections / they know what to attack

why won't she love me, you wonder

as I extract you from the skin
you lodged yourself into uninvited

i n h a b i t a n t

Like the charcoal underneath my fingernails,
I cannot rid you from
making your habitat in every last part of me—
in each crevice and furrow
You plummet into my pores
I find you burrowed into my crow's feet
and lodged inside my tear ducts
You occupy my vessels, veins, arteries
You are present *everywhere*
My breaths reek of your lips;
you cling onto every inhale and exhale

How can I remove you from me?
Would I have to cut off my limbs?
My arms, my legs—
Shed my skin?
Donate every ounce of my blood?
What would it take to rid myself of you?

You have dug into my core,
used it as grounds for your well;
everything I do springs up from you

I don't know how to escape what fuels me

How can I remove you from me?

Would I have to
cut off my limbs?

Shed my skin?

Donate every ounce of my blood?

What would it take to
rid myself of you?

h a i k u

I love you loudly
because of you I am proud
you whisper my name

YOU PLUCKED ME
FROM THE TREE
BEFORE I WAS READY

IT MUST
BE WINTER
FOREVER

WHAT WOULD
IT TAKE TO
RID MYSELF
OF YOU

I'VE YET TO
DISINFECT MY
MEMORY OF THE
SHIFT IN YOUR VOICE

MY FLAME,
IT LOST ITS LIGHT

bitter roots

I haven't been writing
with roots of bitterness lately.

For a while, my words stemmed from hate—
from trauma, from pain—
from being dragged out of the driver's seat
and being told how to behave.
I wasn't allowed to drive my own vehicle,
or have my own thoughts—
instead, I was called names,
and given silent treatments and blame
for doing nothing except give *everything*.

After only overflowing kindness,
I was made to cry for the delight of it—
Car doors were opened for me
only to be degraded once inside
and I slowly began to dwindle,
my flame, it lost its light—
my car became a place of hatred,
so when I had the chance to drive,
I only wanted to escape it—
and I hate to admit that
I thought I'd go off an embankment
to get away from it;
I could yank the wheel
and be saved from this.

But I've always wanted to *live*.
I was naive, only knowing to give—
but I still blame myself
for always choosing to forgive
and not realizing it sooner that
there's more to life than this.

And I want to apologize to my dad
for all of this you've seen—
and for the parts you didn't know,
that now you've had to read.
You've probably wondered if you failed
to exemplify what a man should be.
But Dad, there's never been a man like you.
I've never met a heart so pure, so genuine and true.
And all the words I said from bitter roots,
none of them were true.
I want you to know that I love you.
And one day I'll choose a wonderful man,
but he'll never be as wonderful as you.

love,
ellen

Dear little precious Ellen,

you are such a
wondeful little girl.
I Love you with all my
heart.

your sweet Daddy

a failed attempt at destruction

It's been a while now,
long enough for me to forget most things about you.
But I've yet to disinfect my memory
of the shift in your voice—
Like magma clambering up the walls of a volcano,
eager to burst through the seams of the earth,
your voice foreshadowed an impending eruption
and I was always the villager
scrambling to avoid destruction

But I was never prepared for the catastrophe—
I never was equipped to combat you—
I was scalded by you so many times
I am in awe that my flesh still clings to my bones—
My mind has been blistered
and seared by your sick manipulations
I am in awe that I am not simply a mesh of scar tissue—
I am in awe that my sanity wasn't liquefied,
or left in fragments, or disintegrated

You came with an intent to
belittle and deprecate me—
with an intent to showcase
the hopelessness of my existence
but instead you have proven to me
the magnitude of my strength

If I can withstand the fury of a volcano
I was made to survive anything

You came with an intent

to belittle and deprecate me

with an intent to showcase

the hopelessness of my existence

but instead you have proven to me

the magnitude of my strength

r o t t e n   f r u i t

I am not a fruit for your delight,
and never was; you just used me as such.
I will not allow you again to squelch out the life
I've worked so hard to fill myself up with.

You plucked me from the tree before I was ready,
when I was new and filled with life,
and you sank into me with your nasty teeth—
drained my zest for your own pleasure.
You thought you bettered me, ripened me;
but I was made to rot
and every blemish that appeared,
you were the cause.

But *piece by piece,*
I have cut you out.
And although parts of me are missing,
I salvaged what was left of myself;
buried my seeds back below the ground
where I once began,
and *root by root,*
I clawed my way out of the dark earth.
And as I'm rising from the ground,
seeing the light again for the first time,
I outstretch my arms towards the heavens,
I lift my head towards the sky,
and I bask in the newness of living.

I am not a fruit for your delight,
but my own tree,
audaciously growing,
daring to create life
as if I had never known the meaning of losing.

fortress

It is time for me to dig a moat around my heart;
surround it with soldiers,
burn down the drawbridge.
I've let too many wanderers
barge into my castle,
reside in my quarters,
and feast at my table.
I've chosen to see the good
in too many evil intentions—
I have given to those
who only seek to receive;
who never intend to give in return

My heart is a castle—
not a subway station,
or an airport,
or a ferry boat—
My heart is something to fight for;
to make a home from—
not something to hop aboard
for a fleeting moment
only to leave and disembark from—

My heart is not a passageway,
or ticket to get somewhere;
my heart is a destination.

But I'm bolting the doors
and barring the windows.
So unless you know
how to build a drawbridge,
and unless you can defeat an entire army
and climb a castle wall with your bare hands,
then you can find another table
to feast at.

in wrong places

I don't know,
I have a knack for finding love in the wrong places.
Maybe love will find me in the right one.

PART II

THE SCENIC ROUTE

It felt great to be in control again. My feet pedaled faster and more fervently than ever. My bicycle basket carried a newly gained confidence and a smile. I felt alive again. I couldn't fall if I wanted to. Or so I thought. I didn't fall off of the bicycle this time; but instead, fell for another person. A genuinely good person. Someone who rode along this journey with me, bettering me as we went. Together, we took the scenic route.

You are anything but temporary,
could **never** be forgettable.

fleeting

I have only met you in brief moments;
in passing, in eye contact across the room—
but like smoke that clings onto clothing
you linger on me

I look for you everywhere—
see your face in crowds
where you aren't
hear your voice in places
you've never been
dream up conversations
we haven't had

our encounters have been fleeting
but you are anything but temporary,
could never be forgettable

november 3rd, 2019

The first day I spent time with you,
you spun your thrift store records
while we drew portraits
of each other into our sketchbooks

And in my mind
I wished you were the record player
and I was the vinyl
and that you were spinning me beneath your arm,
dancing around the living room to the music

But all the while
I admired you from across the couch
and I loved you silently
and clung onto the hope that
you were inaudibly loving me too

do i ever cross your mind?

Do I ever cross your mind?
Do I float in, gently, like a feather?
Or do I hit you all at once,
like a tsunami, destructive weather?
Do you think of me on sunlit days
because you're reminded of my light?
Or do you think of me in darkness
because I remind you of the night?

Do I ever cross your mind?
And if I do, what do you see?
I see *you* in everything,
but do you ever think of *me?*

poison ivy

Your poison ivy lips —
I am apprehensive to graze them
in case I should become infected.
They will leave me
itching for you for days
My skin will crawl, ache, swell
from the remnants of you
You will linger here for weeks
My fingertips will become
like magnets to my lips
I will not be able
to resist from tracing them,
trying to mimic the electricity of your touch

Just the thought of kissing you
has me poisoned

feeling colors

We came together,
an uncalculated collision
of lips and skin;
my breaths unsteady
and lips quivering
from the eagerness of wanting you
and the nervousness of
not knowing your lips before
It was far from mathematical
but much like a collision of acrylics
on a blank canvas
ready to meet colors for the first time

I had only seen colors,
never felt them,
until I'd kissed you.

I had only seen colors,
never felt them,
until I'd kissed you.

u n w r i t a b l e b o y,

It is impossible to organize
my thoughts about you.

How can I separate you, divide you, categorize you,
compartmentalize you, formulate you.

How can I place your entire existence
into an arrangement of words
when you dismantle me with your eyes
and unstitch me with your smile
You disassemble me with your laugh
and undo me with your touch

How can I begin to knit together
words to describe you
when you unravel my entire being
with just your presence

How can I begin to knit together
words to describe you
when you unravel my entire being
with just your presence

we embarrassed
the stars, even

We kissed
and you should have seen
the moon and stars
and how they turned their faces
because their eyes
could not handle
the intensity of our light.

mixed signals

my right brain says
you love me.

my left brain is
not that creative.

d e m e n t i a

Please don't fall in love with me
for what I have
or for what I look like when my hair is primped
and when my face is tidied

Fall in love with my unruly hair,
and puffy eyes,
and half-shaven legs
Kiss me with my morning breath
and when I am gray and forget what day it is
and begin to put hairbrushes in the freezer
and dishes in the bathroom
and forget how to brew my evening coffee

Love me and my absent mind,
and when I forget what words to say,
read books to me
and tell me about your day
And when we have the same conversation
three times in a row,
pretend it is new and exciting
so I don't have to remember that I'm forgetting,
so I don't realize that I'm unmaking the memories
that once seemed so secure,
like they would always be there, waiting for me
And above all,
remind me that I am loved.

I don't want to lose myself
without someone there to find me

Kiss me with my morning breath

and when I am gray

and forget what day it is

and begin to put

hairbrushes in the freezer

and dishes in the bathroom

and forget how to brew

my evening coffee

transported

My compass stopped working when you kissed me.
I could have been anywhere. Maybe I lost my senses
or maybe they were amplified. Either way, I was
transported— and I don't want to come back.

e x h i b i t i o n

I am an artist.
You are the only canvas
I want to paint the surface of,
the only palette
I want to dip colors from.

Let me touch you,
I will mold ceramics from your skin
and sculpt abstractions from your lips.
I want to illustrate your
bends and curves with my fingertips.

I am an artist.
I will look into your eyes
and see sapphires—
gaze into your smile
and find amethysts—
place my head upon your chest
and feel rubies between
each of your heartbeats.
I will listen to your emerald laugh
and extract poetry from between each chuckle.

I may be an artist,
but you are the subject
of each and every creation.

Let me make you my favorite exhibition.

one more song

I wish you were a record player
and I was your favorite record.

Place me onto your turntable.
Lower your needle onto my surface,
gently trace along my grooves.
Spin me beneath your arm.
You are the only one
I want to sing melodies for.
Cherish my vinyl carcass.
Tuck me into a sleeve
and protect me from scratches.
I've accumulated too many from careless handlers
who tossed me to the side
into unwanted corners
and onto floorboards in dusty attics.

What if I am stagnant?
What if my only music is static noise?

Show me that I still have a song left to sing

rough draft

I don't want to edit you.
I don't want to mark you out with red ink.
I don't want to manipulate you,
rearrange you, change you.
I don't want to fancy you up,
dull you down, shape you.
I don't want you as anything
except who you are right now.
I want you for *you.*
Your rough draft.

```
ROUGH DRAFT

I don't want to edit you.
I don't want  to to mark you out with red ink.
I don't want to manipulate you,
rearrange you, change you.
I don't want to fancy you up,
dull you down, shape you.
I don't want you as anything
except who you are right now.
I want you for you.
Your rough draft.
```

vincent please don't gogh

Please do not be *Vincent*;
don't *Gogh* because you think you've not been loved.
Since the *Starry Night* I met you,
my smile's beamed brighter than the heavens above.

I think of us in *The Night Cafe,*
when you first caught me with your gaze—
and of our days beneath the *Cypress* tree
sharing warmth beneath the shade.

I keep your *Sunflowers* on my dresser;
I'll keep them long after they're dead.
They remind me of our walks in *Daubigny's Garden*
beneath the sun that kissed our heads.

I've loved you for infinity;
I hope this doesn't reach you late—
I want to get the chance to tell you
before we meet at *Eternity's Gate.*

I've loved you

for infinity;

I hope this doesn't

reach you late

t a n g l e d

I don't know what
it is that I'm captivated by
when it comes to you—
Despite the times you've
tried to push me away,
I have loved you.

You are magnetic,
even when you are not
Even on days when
the world's weight is insufferable
and you think your existence
only adds to the heaviness of it,
you are still magnetic—
and I am still drawn to you

Even at your worst,
I am a moth
willingly tangled in your web
and I would purposely fling myself into it
again and again
if it meant giving you
the strength for another tomorrow

if i say, "i love you,"

Love hurts because it can be lost
and because it can be forged to begin with.

"I love you" is too effortlessly slipped from lips.
It is undemanding.
It is simple to say, but challenging to mean.
It glides off crooked tongues
and anchors itself onto honest ones.
It is painless to say with deceit
and strenuous to say with sincerity.

I want to say "I love you," but only if I can say it wholly.
If I say, "I love you," I want it to be unrelated to time,
and measured only by the joining of your heart and mine,
the moment when two lives become one.

dear mr. glass half-empty,

You worry I see you for what you're not—
for the past decisions you have made
and the sufferings they've brought.

And though you're far from yielding fruit,
I see a sprout emerging from the pot;
a flower knowing it can bloom,
he simply just forgot.

And maybe I don't mean much to you,
but you're a universe to me.
And though you can see your ending,
I see a boundless infinity

of a genuine kindness,
not selfishness or greed—
a wish to better yourself, and in return,
you better everyone you meet.

But when the day meets its end,
you can't find yourself through me.
And as much as I'd like to show you,
it's your own discovery.

I can tell you of your worth,
but only you can set it free.
And maybe you would spread your wings
if you saw what I can see.

love,
ms. glass half-full

if you kiss a wound

They say, *If you kiss a wound it will heal*—
but I can't kiss your heart.
So I'll kiss your lips, your neck, your skin,
and every other part.
And I hope that one day they'll sink in
and something inside you starts—
because where you see yourself as worthless,
all I see is a work of art.

So I'll begin to paint your canvas
with the stain from on my lips.
and I will trace your frame so gently,
from your torso to your hips.
I'll leave landscapes on your body;
there's not a place that I will miss.
And I'll always be here to remind you
in case you should forget.

But if life ever comes between us,
or if mine comes to an end,
I hope that at the very least,
when you needed me, I was a friend.
And I hope that if I've shown you anything,
it's that every wound can mend—
that your life is far from meaningless;
you hold universes within.

Know that you can do anything you fathom,
if you only would believe.
And the gift of happiness awaits you,
if you're willing to receive.
And there's so much love around you—
more than you can conceive.
But I hope you find it in yourself,
before it's time for you to leave.

b a r e

Sometimes I have to remind myself
that you are real
and not a fabrication
of my incessant imagination—
Sometimes I feel like I could blink
and you would disappear
but I open my eyes
and you are always standing here
showing me what it means
to be loved for myself
and not for the woman I could be
if I was born as someone else
and had lovelier locks of hair
or seamless skin

But you love me, bare—
the way we are all meant to be loved—
stripped of all the excess
that we put upon ourselves
and then wonder why we are
weighed down and heavy
You love me, bare—
cleansed of makeup,
frills, and material goods

You love me, bare—
and I have become
light and weightless;
free from gravity almost

You love me, bare--

and I have become

light and weightless;

free from gravity almost

together

You make me think of things
like blueprints and yellow houses,
fenced-in yards and wrap-around porches,
car seats and tiny shoes

I have always been afraid
of tomorrows, and leaving my twenties,
and misplacing my memories—
but you make me think of things
like growing old in rocking chairs,
forgetting the world together

let me write you into a poem

Let me write you into a poem. Let me clothespin you
onto the blue lines of the paper, iron you into the space
between the margins, and string you into words that
could somehow immortalize you.

Let me write you into a poem.
And just maybe, I'll be there too.

f r e e d o m

The most freedom I've found
has never been from
places my feet have roamed
or in building blocks of
places I've called home—
I have not found it
in the confines of walls,
or boundary lines,
or the atmosphere even—
that itself is not freeing enough for me

I love the flower fields
and the tides of the oceans
and the cliffs etched into mountaintops
and yet I've not found
a field freckled with enough flowers
or a seaside blanketed with blue enough waters
or a mountain with tall enough peaks
to compare with the freedom
I find in your arms

Like a black hole,
I fall into you;
gravity rips me apart
at your smile
and I'm completely satisfied
with the thought
of never escaping you

like a black hole,
I fall into you;
gravity rips me apart
at your smile
and I'm completely okay
with the thought
of never escaping you

a patient gardener

Dear gardener,

You have seen me at my worst.
You uproot the weeds I find myself tangled in.
And when my blooms are spent and heavy,
you cut them off, diligently,
to encourage new ones to grow in their place.
You have seen me in drought,
my limbs limp and shriveled
and deprived of nutrients.
You have seen me in wilt,
and still you tend to me,
believing that tomorrow I will rise again.
You find promise in my tomorrows
and love me for my imperfect todays.

Dear gardener,
I do not deserve the care
of your calloused and tender hands.

You find promise in my tomorrows

and love me for my imperfect todays.

my final sunrise

I don't think kissing should grow stale with age.
Who says that growing older means growing farther apart?
I refuse for doom to sit comfortably at my table.

I want to grow hopelessly intertwined with someone.
I hope my lover knows laughter and shares it well.
Who has time to worry about wrinkles?
They are a small price to pay for years of fulfillment.
I hope my face becomes a grand canyon of them all
so I know I have experienced uncontained joy with someone.
Then, I will know I have lived well.

When I come to the end of my life,
and the sun greets me one final morning,
I hope to be cluelessly happy,
obliviously enthusiastic,
and too preoccupied with the zeal of life
to notice something as trivial as death coming for me.
I hope to start my final morning
like every one of my other mornings.
I will roll over and give my lover a kiss.

silence

It is the quiet hours
that are my favorites with you—
It is the moments of stillness,
when silence settles in
and the room is dim,
but your eyes are not

It is in these quiet moments with you
that my love for you is the loudest.

we don't have to do anything

We don't have to do anything;
being with you is enough.

We could sit at the kitchen table for hours
looking at computer screens
and paper-ridden dreams;
or we could venture the world,
partake in all the finer things

We could do anything, or nothing at all,
and I would feel as if we were dangling our feet
off the edge of the atmosphere,
looking at the world below us,
but forgetting that it exists

the two of us is all I see;
where we go or what we do,
it's only you and me.

"i love you."

I love you. Here it exists in writing and still, it doesn't compare to how I truly feel for you. It looks misspelled, but it isn't— it just wades shallow compared to the depths of my affection towards you. You've changed me like the sun changes the world each morning. You've become so interlaced with me that I don't know how I ever lived without you.

I love you.
I love you like the earth loves to spin.
Like the leaves meet the wind.
I love you like lilies love valleys.
I love you.
I love you like every example of love possible,
except nothing like those examples; *not even close.*
I love you and I always will.

y o u

You are the sun to my day
and the moon to my night—
You take all of my darkness
and turn it to light

if my heart is a landscape

I love you, I do.
My love, it has always been you.
If my heart is a landscape,
then *you* are the view.
You turn my darkness to light;
my steel gray to blue.
When prisms bring rainbows,
you are *every* hue.
You are the song of the sparrows,
the ballad of the bees.
You are the dance of the dandelions,
you are the wind in the trees.
You are in every valley of my soul,
in every mountain and each peak.
You are my fountain of strength
in the times I am weak.

You are genuine good
in a world where good remains few.
You bring life to my landscape;
you make this aged heart feel new.
But you're *more* than a scenery;
you're more than a view.
You're more than a rhyme could conjure,
more than a line could construe—
You are more than what letters could describe,
more than what numbers could ever accrue.
But of this one thing I'm certain—
and this will forever ring true—
My dearest love, *I will always love you.*

If my heart is a landscape,

then you are the view.

let's

There are too many ways
to say, "I love you."
and not enough time to say them all

So let's just take the evening slow
and make the most of it—
Let's split a sundae, share the sunset,
and simply sit
in the stillness of our love
watching the world whirl around us, and above—

Let's linger in the last of the day,
and let the clock hands carry our worries away—
and everything
except our love for each other

Let's let love stay

there are too many ways
to say I love you
and not enough time
to say them all
so let's take the evening
slow and make the most of
it

let's spit a sundae and
share the sunset together
+ ~~simply~~ sit in the
stillness of our love
while watching the
world whirl around us

let's take on the last
of the day
and forget about time
together

my favorite place

I want to capture you on paper
in the same way a camera could on a screen
I wish I could press a button
and you'd appear in a perfect arrangement of words
I wish I could put my heart through a scanner—
maybe then, I could describe you
and the way you make me feel—
but how can I put words to feelings
my heart has never felt before?

How can I condense you down into a page, or two,
or two thousand—
when looking at you
is enough to stir oceans out of my eyes—
not because you make me unhappy,
but because out of everywhere I've been,
you are my favorite place to be—
and when I look at you I wonder
how you aren't the highlight of everyone's day
or how your name isn't etched into a monument
or at least put on a street sign yet—
or how *maybe I'm not really in the Milky Way*
and maybe you and I aren't really
just sitting on a bed
in a room where you can't see the carpet from all the clothes
or make it to the bathroom without tripping—

because being with you
feels like I am in another universe
and you are simply sitting in front of me,
looking down at something you are working on,
unknowingly bringing tears to my eyes
by doing nothing except
cross-legged and effortlessly
being my everything

our love language is braille

You speak to me with your hands
and I listen to you with mine
You run your fingers over me
like I am Braille;
starting with the title on my spine,
then exploring further—
reading me like
a cliffhanger lies on
every   inch   of   my   skin

You are always reaching for the next word
and I do the same with you—
like each touch will solve a mystery—
but our plot always meets a twist,
and these lovely pages never end

We are lost
along the lines in our story
where every word is different
but all of them are exclaiming, "I love you."

i have never loved february

I have never loved February,
but I love how much you love February;
how your eyes light up
when the world is a snow globe
and we are just two figurines
watching the sky shake snowflakes from the clouds

I have never loved February,
so I am hoping they disappear
as soon as they touch the ground,
but you are holding onto every flake
like they are trophies sent to you from God—
and the only reason I understand it
is because I am holding onto you
for the very same reason

a letter to a lover

I don't know how to tell you that I love you, perhaps because three words could never justify exactly how I feel for you. So maybe four words can describe how I feel a little more accurately.

You are my universe. The dictionary says that the universe is all of space, and time, and their contents. So, in other words, the universe is everything. You are my everything. When you look up at the stars, can you imagine their end? I imagine constellations after constellations, galaxies after galaxies. I cannot picture the sky ever coming to a point where the stars cease to exist and there is a sudden wall of infinite blackness. I imagine the stars going on forever. My love for you is the same. It continues on and on and on.

When I tell you that you are my universe, I am not saying that everything will always be perfect. Even the brightest stars fall from the sky. Some explode. Some burn out. But amidst all of our explosions and shortcomings and falling outs, *I will still love you.* Because out of all of the things that fail in this life, love never does.

You are my universe. But even those four words do not unravel my love for you; I'm not sure if anything ever will.

Even the brightest stars

fall from the sky.

Some explode.

Some burn out.

But amidst all of our explosions

and shortcomings and falling outs,

I will still love you.

l o s t

Our eyes are filled with mysteries
and universes never discovered

and there is someone for each of us
willing to risk everything
for a chance to get lost in their wonder
and uncover our heart's greatest secrets

OUR EYES ARE FILLED
WITH MYSTERIES

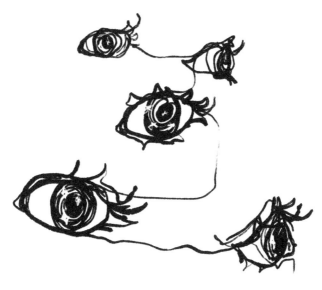

UNIVERSES
NEVER DISCOVERED

tailor of my heart

You're the tailor of my heart;
before I met you, I was worn.
A gaping hole lay beneath my chest
from all the times I had been torn.

You're the tailor of my heart;
You took out your needles and your thread.
You stitched life into the parts of me
I'd long since thought were dead.

You're the tailor of my heart;
The first stitch had a bit of sting,
But you carried on with gentle patience,
weaving love into my being.

You're the tailor of my heart;
slowly, my heart began to sing.
This winter I'd been buried in
took its first breath of spring.

You're the tailor of my heart;
it is you who made me whole.
It is *you* who now is woven
into each fiber of my soul.

You're the tailor of my heart,
but you're also my *best friend*.
You loved me when I was broken,
and I'll love you until my end.

You stitched life
into the parts of me
I'd long since
thought were dead.

where willowbrook ends

I have gotten to know you best
after midnight
underneath muted kitchen lights
and between ceaseless conversations
and comfortable silence

I have gotten to know you best
during early morning back massages
and while listening to stand-up comedians
who hardly make me laugh as much as you do

I have gotten to know you best
listening to you recite your poems
and watching you carefully craft each sentence
until the weight of your words
moves us both to tears

I have gotten to know you best
by your daily interactions
and from the way you invest your time
into making everyone around you feel seen
even when *you* feel invisible

I have gotten to know you best
sitting together in plastic chairs
on a dead-end street
where Willowbrook ends and our love began

And as it continues to live on,
I will continue to praise God
for investing his time
into creating the one
who I am *proud* to know best

I have gotten to know you best
from these things and more
and from looking into your green eyes
and forgetting that any other color exists

unclouded soul

My arms are wrapped around your waist,
I never want to let you go.
It's not your body that I'm holding;
it's your pure, unclouded soul.
It's not your skin, it's what's within—
your heart and mine have joined so close.
This love we've built together
never fails to overflow.

You've been such a privilege to know.
I never want to let you go.

It's not your body
that I'm holding;
it's your pure, unclouded soul.

a love like rain

Although I hope it doesn't,
if this ever ends,
at least I will know
that I loved you like rain, except better
I didn't freeze
when the cold seasons
nipped at the passion between us—
Didn't allow myself
to harden in your presence—
Would never allow my words
to become stiff—
only let them pitter-patter gently
from the roof of my mouth
and land on your ears lovingly

I've loved you like rain,
but not with the intent to drown you—
just soak you lightly,
enough to keep you nurtured
and thriving in the sunlight
and you have loved me the same

And if this is to end,
we will know that it wasn't because
we have been unkind to one another—

We just happened to have been planted
next to each other,
and we grew together happily—
sharing each other's nutrients,
and soaking in the same radiant sun—
but our roots were simply meant for different soils,
and that's okay.

Together, we grew in the right direction.
We sprung forth in flowers.
We brought color to the world.
We were happy.

Although I hope it doesn't happen,
if someone else sees me in full bloom,
it was you who helped me blossom—
and I'll always be grateful for that.

evening thoughts on love

I don't care about games— the cat and mouse chase of keeping someone in love. I don't believe love is something that can be forced upon someone or begged for. If someone loves you, they'll make sure you know it. If they don't, maybe that means something.

When I was a child, we had a pet toad for a winter. We would dangle ham and cheese from a string and make a game out of feeding him. Many times I remember pulling the string away from him right as he lunged for a bite. The tantalizing was fun. It was a thrill to see him work harder for his meals.

But I won't dangle my love before you. I have never been someone to withhold my affection for the sake of being pursued. I don't believe love is something that can be half-done. I will love you whole-heartedly and will remind you of my feelings often. I don't know how to constrain a feeling that is so powerful. I also don't know why I'd want to suppress it, after seeing how beatific and plentiful love is when it is shared with someone.

I guess I could show my love less if I wanted to protect myself. Maybe when I've parted ways with people it could have helped ease the blow a little. Maybe if I had given less of myself, it wouldn't have been as painful to find myself again.

But I've never been good at pretending not to love someone.

Anyways, even if I was, I'm sure I'd always wonder if I could have given more, and the uncertainty would be just as agonizing. So when it comes to you, I'll do the only thing I know to do. I'll love you and make sure you know it.

the ending of things

In the end of it all,
when it is time for us
to blow out the stars
that we lit together like candles,
I hope you remember me
with a spirit like evergreens—
undisturbed by the brisk and frigid seasons
that have a tendency to turn life into death—
and know that I've always
wished the same for you

And when life greets you with hostility,
I hope you remember my love
draping around you
like a warm summer evening;
a reminder of the comfort love can bring.
And although we burned bright together,
I hope the light you shine on your own
burns much brighter,
and the love you find proves much stronger,
and I hope you are overtaken by a happiness
that makes you forget about any sadness—
a happiness that makes every other joy seem dull

When life greets you

with hostility,

I hope you remember

my love draping around you

like a warm summer evening

valentine's day

It's Valentine's Day and honestly I'm not feeling too loved. I know I am loved, but today I am tired. There are so many things I need to do, and I don't have the motivation to move. I've just been in bed. I want to get up and work on my personal projects. I have art to make and words to write and people to say "I love you" to. But I've not had any motivation today. I went to get a cheese pizza for myself and the car took forever to defrost. It finally warmed up and I drove to the pizza shop feeling completely alone. *I was alone.*

It has been quiet today. Sometimes I wonder if I've ever really been in love. I know I have loved; there is no doubt about that. I've poured my entire soul into people and have given so much of myself. And I know that I'm far from perfect. But today is one of those days that I'm thinking about the lengths I go to make people smile and I'm driving in silence. I forgot to play music and that scares me too because I always love listening to music. I don't know why I'm rambling. I just need to think out loud sometimes. I wish I could get up and start working because I know at the end of the day, it would be worth it. But I'm just so tired and feeling unloved.

disconnected

I have been feeling a little disconnected
from you lately.

Like a radio station starting to lose signal—
like a melody becoming static.

Like a shortage in my aux cord—
in every direction I turn, I can't find clarity.
Everything is fuzzy here
in our world that used to be so clear.

Like poor cell service.

Like I'm the one bulb in a strand of string lights
that flickers out and makes the rest go dim.

Like "we" doesn't sound like "we" anymore.
but more like "me"
and more like "you"
and less like "us."

I have been feeling a little disconnected lately and
I don't know how to keep the signal from getting weaker.

tree of life and death

I've seen the trees; I know what they do.
I know their cycle of revival—
how they empty themselves
of their leaves just to rejuvenate again—
I know it should inspire me,
seeing them resurrect after death,
seeing them fill themselves
after seasons of emptiness,
but the leaves won't stop taunting me.
Leave. They say.
Leave!
We do it everyday! It's what we are!

"It's not that easy," I grumble.
I've never been good at letting go—
at letting something I've grown with
fall away from me;
but I do it for the sake of myself.
I have to live; I have to let go of all that's dying
or all that is meant to.
I have to leave.
I know I'm always talking in analogies.
I think it's easier for me to make sense of things.

I have to live;

I have to let go of all that's dying

or all that is meant to.

I have to leave.

PART III

USING THE BRAKES

Unfortunately, even the scenic route can be riddled with potholes, freckled with boulders, and filled with unpredictable twists and turns. As a cyclist navigating these roads, we are forced to make decisions. We have to use our best judgment to maneuver through the obstacles that lie ahead of us. Sometimes, we have to switch gears. We have to use the brakes.

When it comes to loving and letting go of love, using the brakes is never easy. Sometimes, it feels nearly impossible. The jolt can be devastating, and at times, unbearable. Sometimes, it will be so painful that we will wonder if we'll ever be able to move forward again. But I'd rather experience a sudden halt in my path than allow myself to ride through a pothole or crash into a boulder. I'd rather stop myself short than continue riding down a road that only grows ruttier and more treacherous. Sometimes, the scenic route starts looking less scenic. Sometimes, a love meant to last forever is actually temporary. At the end of the day, I have to put myself first. I have to strap my self-worth into the bicycle basket and guard it for dear life. I had already lost control of the pedals, once. I didn't plan on losing control of the brakes, too. Unfortunately, using the brakes has been something I have become very familiar with.

changes

But instead I will be
someone else's forever,
and infinity does not feel
eternal without him.

keepsake

It doesn't feel real that this is ending.
This moment with you,
I wish I could stay in it forever.
I'd swallow it if I could;
press it like wildflowers
into the holiest book of my mind as a keepsake
and hope that it stays
preciously preserved between the pages
so I always remember us beautiful
and our love strong.
You've always been so good to me.

And when life greets me with bitterness,
I'll flip back through these pages
until it stops on the wildflowers.
And even though they will have faded,
their petals wrinkled and dried
and broken off into the binding,
there will always be a hint of color
reminding me of what it felt like
to be alive with you.
Reminding me of your smile.
And of your heart like the ocean;
always full, always giving to the shore
and pulling away—
only to give more of yourself again.
You've always been so selfless.

It doesn't feel real that this is ending,
but I'll let the book close on this moment;
inside each other's arms,
my head on your heartbeat,
holding each other tightly
as if we weren't about to let go.

one of our last days

We sat on the edge of the rocks and watched the great golden yolk slip out of the sky, ending with the same splendor it began with. Its final moments were captured in orange glints on the water's surface that slid over the edge of the dam and collapsed into more of itself. I thought about the river; how nice it must be to not have to *think* about anything—it all simply flows together in one harmonious body; nothing is left out or disjointed. Everything drifts together and not apart from. *I wish everything worked that way. I wish endings didn't exis*—

my wishes were interrupted as the sun's reflection left the river— then, we climbed off of the rocks, walked to the car, and closed the door—leaving the river behind us and entering into the dark night.

a great day with you

I had a great day with you, I always do.
That's why it hurts so much to know
the day is almost through; it's our last.
I hate the way time glides on so fast.
I wish I could linger longer in this moment,
but in a blink, it's in the past.
I had a great day with you, I always do.
I wish I could go back.

tonight i wish
i had more time

What kind of moon is this tonight?
What kind of moon is hanging
in the wardrobe of this midnight sky?
It's our goodnight moon, our goodbye moon;
the last moon with your hand in mine.
Two years of moons have come and gone,
but tonight I wish I had more time.
I wish I could steer the moon off course,
tell the stars to unalign.
Tonight I wish I had more time.
More "I love you's," more "love you too's,"
your heartbeats next to mine.
More silent conversations,
singing love songs with our eyes.
I am going to miss you,
this moon will soon say its last "goodnight."

The day brings all that's good and bright,
but I dread to see the morning light.

I wish I could steer the moon off course,
tell the stars to unalign.

Tonight I wish I had more time.

packing

You're moving boxes, I'm watching.
It is time for you to leave.
This mountain of belongings you're taking with you
is *far less* than all you've left with me.

You've given me laughter
and a joy beyond compare.
You've given me encouragement
in times when *no one else* was there.
You've reminded me of my self-worth
when I struggled to simply see;
You've grounded me in moments
the world was slipping from beneath my feet.

You've given me your soul;
the purest heart I've ever known.
It's not this house I'm going to miss;
it's this man who has been my home.
As cardboard cubes fill up this "living" room,
my heart sinks into vacancy.
I don't know how I'm going to *live*
without the one who makes me, "me."

the last goodbye

How do you condense an entire relationship with someone into one final moment? How do you cram everything you want to say into a goodbye? How are you supposed to condense the years you thought you'd spend with someone into a short summary with an abrupt ending? How do you break a soul-tie?

How are you supposed to just end something like that?

"f r o n t d o o r"

Outside these doors,
couples are laughing;
people in love and choosing each other
Inside these doors,
a couple is weeping;
two people in love and choosing to be apart
I keep hoping that one day we will wake up
and things will be different,
but we already *are* different
and this hairline-thread of difference
feels like mountains between us—
yet I'm so close to you
it's like we are woven into one skin

I try to hold onto you—
your cheeks, your hands
your arms, your legs,
your shoes, even—
still it isn't enough to keep you here
inside these doors
It isn't enough to keep the birch branches
from flailing against the brick and gutters
and knocking on the door of this temporary house,
urging you to come outside

We know the birch tree is right,
but wish it wouldn't be—
wish the wind wasn't calling
us away from each other

But we walk out,
painfully listening
to the *wind whispering loudly*
and the *sirens screaming quietly*
and the *trees tapping impatiently*
and the *headlights hurrying idly*
and the *world whirling around us quickly,*
but slower than I've ever experienced

For a moment it all feels bearable
because we are outside of these doors together
and being with you has always felt like
the calm in every storm

But it is a fleeting moment;
a last kiss, a last grab of the hand,
a last look of acknowledgement
Both of us pleading into each others' eyes
while feeling known and understood
by each other for the last time—
afraid of being strangers, afraid of being lovers—

and now I am inside these doors
trying not to curse at God
and trying to accept that
this front door is meant to stand between us

and now I am inside these doors
~~things fa~~ trying not to curse at God
~~the for you being outside~~
~~trying~~ not to lose myself
~~trying not to~~.

this hairline
thread of difference

feels like mountains

between us

yet I'm so close to you
it's like we are woven
into one skin.

if it falls off its axis

I know the world is spinning.

I am reminded because the sun continues to pry
my eyelids apart in the mornings
and the birdsongs mingle with my ears
hoping to wrangle me out of my bedsheets
and the trees empty themselves
of their leaves just to fill them back up again—

I know it should inspire me,
knowing that I can do the same,
knowing that my winter is here only for a season.
I know.

I know the world is spinning.
But I don't care if it continues to spin
or if it loses its balance
and topples off of its axis

The world may be spinning,
but if you aren't here
to dance with me while it turns,
my world might as well not be spinning at all.

morning breath

I could be angry at the morning.
I could spit at the sun for daring to rise
and shed light on this bed
where you aren't and never will be.

I could be angry at the morning
for beginning with the sun instead of you
and for waking me up with light
instead of your lips.

I could be angry at the morning.
I could be—and I want to be—
but I would rather walk outside,
exhale my morning breath,
and inhale the beginning of this beautiful day.

remains

The ramen bowls
are piling up, scattered
across my room
like mines in a minefield
I can't bring myself
to carry them to the sink,
pour them empty.
The bathtub water
has been filled for days
For some reason
I can't bring myself
to pull the faucet
and let it drain.
Everything is dirty here
in this room
I've found so much love in
I'm a mess and
I can't bring myself
to rinse off;
don't want to erase
your touch from my skin
your kisses from my lips
your hands from my hair
Everything remains the same
and nothing is the same at all
I can't bring myself
to purge the remnants of you

How do I move on from love
when I don't want to
I'm holding onto the last of you
while knowing I have to let go

the mourning

It's so difficult mourning someone. Even though they aren't dead, it feels like they are. The worst part about losing someone is that they are still in reach, but you have to force yourself to stay away. Conceal the car keys so you don't drive to where they are. Put away the pictures. Hide things that remind you of them so you can forget and move on. Forgetting is the worst part. Especially when you don't want to forget them. But to move on, you do forget. You forget what things they said that made you belly laugh. Your inside jokes drift to the outside. They fade from memory. You can look back at pictures but forget what happened during that moment. Forget what other things you did that day. What conversations you had. It all just—fades.

all of the empty spaces

You are the gap between my fingers
and the leg I still reach for in my passenger seat
You are the silence where music used to play
and the opening between my lips

You are all of the empty spaces that complete me
and I am *completely empty*

e n g u l f e d

If you're asking around,
I'm down by the sea.
Waters surround me;
sands encompass my feet.

I know you're leaving
without a goodbye;
on top of these waters,
but under this sky.

So I'll let these waves
sweep up my cage;
toss me and turn me
in all of their rage.

They won't bring me to you,
but at least I'll remain
in the place where you left,
and here I will stay.

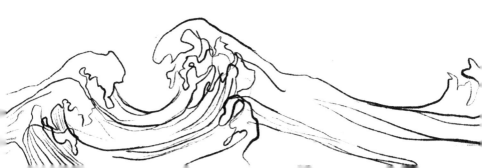

loving you quietly

I don't know how to talk about you without crying
or say, "I don't love you" without lying,

so I am quiet these days.

the lotus pond

I sit at a different side of the pond now
and watch the ducks waddle along the bank
where we used to sit
The pond is even more beautiful
than when we left it
It was the end of May
and the end of us too—
the pond was bare, then

June is coming to a close,
and already, everything is beginning
to bloom and open—
The lotus pads
freckle the cheeks of the water's surface
and the baby turtles freckle
the cheeks of the lotus pads

One brave flower is rising above
the water in front of me;
its petal whites grinning in the sunlight
while the mouths of the other lotus are closed—
not quite ready to speak yet

I sit at a different side of the pond now,
and everything is more beautiful
than when we left it
but still, it's underwhelming

I don't want to watch the ducks by myself
or laugh at the kids catching minnows
and squealing, "it's humongous!"
I don't want the red fox to come back
without you here to see it

I sit at a different side of the pond now,
and the view is disappointing—
and it has nothing to do with what side of the pond I'm on

f o s s i l s

The sun is kissing my face,
and already I think I'm forgetting
what your lips felt like here—
I don't know why; your affection was always so special
and so were you. You *are* special.
I'm trying to hold onto you;
preserve you in thoughts, in words, in art—
in every way I know how—
yet it isn't enough to detain you
from fading away from me.
But even when our conversations and memories
become buried beneath new ones,
and I can no longer remember
the glimmer in your eyes when you
would wait for me in your doorway—
When I am no longer an archaeologist
lucky enough to study the relics in your cheeks—
When my mind becomes weathered and eroded by time
and I can no longer excavate
how it felt to kiss you—
my heart will still know you.

You have engraved your mark on me forever.
You are my favorite fossil in this heart full of remnants,
and traces of you will continue to bring life to me
long after you've left.
Our love is immortalized within me,
and my heart has been restored
simply by knowing you.

You are my favorite fossil

in this heart full of remnants

missing you

Does it hurt as much for you
as it does for me?
The missing you
is a weighted blanket.
My heart crawls under it
and struggles to get up in the morning.
Throughout the day, I am reminded
that it didn't get up from under it at all.
I was laughing today and my stomach ached,
but I barely noticed
because the ache in my heart was far greater.
From the missing you
but forcing myself to not talk to you.
From the thinking of you
but forcing myself to
not think of how I love you
and how I want to see you again.
I could be doing anything
and the back of my mind
is whispering your name.

My heart is blanketed
by the heaviness of missing you
and I don't know when
I'll feel free again
or if I even want to

forgetting

I miss you more than anything
I miss my laugh, too—
I haven't heard it in a while
and I'm starting to forget what it
sounds like to be happy
but I don't want to hear it
come back for anyone else

I wonder if you miss me too
or if you've forgotten me
the same way I've forgotten myself

irreversible

I know you have seen reversible jackets—
the kind you can flip inside out
and each side is completely different from the other

I wish I could do the same with my heart
I wish I could simply flip it inside out —
maybe the new side wouldn't be broken
and weathered and wrinkled
I wish I could say
the damage my heart has sustained
is reversible

Now that I have given my love away,
I just want to ask for it back
Next time, I'd keep it with me;
maybe then, I would have some left to give to someone

How can I ever love someone again
when I barely have enough left for myself

Now that I have given my love away,

I just want to ask for it back

Next time, I'd keep it with me;

maybe then, I would have some left

to give someone

to break a home

Your laptop is singing an 8 hour loop of
To Build A Home by the Cinematic Orchestra
while we are painting in the kitchen
and I'm throwing a paintbrush, grabbing paper towels
and wildly wiping acrylics off my canvas
while you calmly wipe tears from my cheeks
All I can see are mistakes;
nothing I do is good enough for myself,
but it's more than enough for you—
you always see the best in me.
You are just happy to create next to me.

We wanted to have fun that day.
All I can think back on is my anger
and my competitive spirit
intruding on a peaceful evening
and me missing moments I should have kissed you
Should have told you I loved you more
when I had the chance
But your patient heart loved me through it
told me my yellow smears looked great anyway—
those uneven splotches plastering the canvas—
and I'm lying here on another sleepless night
with the painting shoved in my closet
so I don't have to look at it
But I'm wanting another painting day with you
Wanting a redo
Wanting to turn back time
to hold you for one more second of that 8 hour loop
and hoping the clock hands get stuck there

NOTHING I DO IS GOOD ENOUGH
FOR MYSELF BUT IT IS
MOR̶... ...KNOUGH FOR YOU

NOUGH

IS

YOU

HING

OR

RE T

NOTHING I DO IS GOOD ENOUGH
FOR MYSELF BUT IT IS
MORE THAN ENOUGH FOR YOU

from everything
to every thing

How does someone begin
as a best friend
and then a lover
but become a box
buried in a drawer
beneath some clothes
inside a closet
behind a door
that rarely opens

How does someone begin
as your *everything*
but end up as
every thing else

m e d u s a

I can't avoid breaking those who encounter me
I unintentionally desolate them
Turn people into wastelands
Fill them only to leave them barren
Reside in them just to leave them vacant

Is this what Medusa feels like
when everything she looks at hardens into stone
Little do they know
I destroy myself
at the thought of wounding someone else

births and deaths

The windows are rolled down
and I'm driving fifty in February
with my left hand thrusted out the window
flailing against the cold
so I can feel something
besides missing you

I miss you like May
and the way you make me feel warm
when everyone around me
feels like December

You are May and June
and July and August
You are all of my favorite times of the year
but even my least favorite months
have been irreplaceable
simply because you were in them

But with the birth of a new year
came the death of ours—

How can it be that we meet our end in January
when the rest of the world is beginning

I miss you like May
and the way you make me feel warm
when everyone around me
feels like December

from my side of the table

Every time you greet my mind,
it wanders to where we both began;
at different sides of your kitchen table—
sharing stories, holding hands.
We moved counter-clockwise around your table,
gradually changing seats with time;
until we made a two-year orbit around your kitchen,
a journey I'm proud to say was mine.
I loved each side of the table;
in every chair, I learned you more.
With learning you, a love grew
that I had never known before.

From the first side of the table,
the wall held stories of your past;
delicate graphite drawings sketched from
bruised knuckles— hands scarred and bashed.
Marilyn, the Mad Hatter,
a dragon, a California tattoo;
each echoes of your younger self—
a life only known by you.

From the second side of the table,
appeared another corner of the room;
it was here I watched your dreams emerge
from root to petaled bloom.
Empty easels began holding canvases,
empty canvases began holding painted scenes—
interpretations for words you'd woven
from the deepest fibers of your being.

From the third side of the table,
behind you, blinked an oven light
whose times always seemed to remind us
that it was hours after midnight.
It was here I began to learn you best;
watched you write, listened to you recite.
Until your words—once shadowed with darkness—
when spoken, now filled the room with light.
Our hearts, as well, were weightless—
free from gravity and bound by love's delight.

From the fourth side of the table,
the counter held a kitchen sink
that proudly drained the leftovers
of the people we used to be.
While flourishing with each other,
we also grew separately.
We made each other better;
became the people we wanted to be.
So that's why this side of the table
has a view that's bittersweet—
because we made it back to where we first began,
but our orbit was complete.

I love each side of your table;
each side brought a different view.
But from every side of the table,
my favorite part was always *you.*
As we stand up from this table,
push in our chairs, and venture apart,
know you'll always hold *the dearest seat*
in the table of my heart.

betrayal

We are not together anymore
and it still feels like a betrayal
to give anyone else
the smile I gave you.

nobody knows me like you

You're the only person
I know how to talk to when things get rough
Sometimes we don't talk at all;
you just hold me and that's enough

But I can't talk to you now.
I just lie here alone without a sound.

I've been here for myself my whole life
and it's been painful, but I've survived.
I'm barely breathing sometimes,
but I'm here, I'm still alive—
still hoping for the morning light.

It's just another painful night.

p r o b a b l y

You're probably painting.
You're probably bringing ideas to life like you always do.
You're probably thinking deeply about everything.
You're probably making everyone around you laugh.
You're probably as beautiful and bright as always
and you probably don't realize it.
You're probably lighting up every room you walk into.

I'm probably wishing I could be in your light,
and you're probably not thinking of me,
not even for a second.

And you're probably not
thinking of me,
not even for a second.

my side of the hourglass

I miss you already and you've barely left.

We keep trying to prolong this;
extend this one more time,
but our time has been spent—
and we cannot keep turning over this hourglass
and falling into each other
while knowing we aren't going anywhere—
when we will always be trapping ourselves
into one end of this hourglass
that we both aren't completely content with
Though we blend together so beautifully—
Though I would stay here for a lifetime if I could—
Would pour myself into your side of the glass forever
if I wasn't sifting pieces of myself to get there—
Would love you for infinity
if I didn't miss my side of the glass
I left behind for you—

Believe me when I say I love you—
but in loving you
I'm leaving pieces of myself behind
and loving myself less

Believe me when I say I love you --

but in loving you

I'm leaving pieces of myself behind

and loving myself less

"g o o d b y e"

I feel like I should say another "goodbye"
to remind myself, *this is the end.*
I haven't seen much "good"
come from our "byes,"
but until I do, I'll just pretend.

I don't see you in every day and night sky.
I don't look for you when cars like yours pass by.
I don't smile at the thought of you,
and afterwards, I don't begin to cry.
I don't wonder how your days have been,
I don't notice your absence from mine.
I don't hope to see your name light up my phone,
I don't wait up in case it might.
I don't ever look out my window
and wish to see you standing there—
with open arms and an open heart
for only you and I to share.
I don't write any words about you,
I don't feel the need to preserve you in my art.
I don't think of you in almost
every second we're apart.

I don't see you in anything,
and I don't feel like I should say goodbye.
But this isn't truth or dare,
and everything I wish was true is all a lie.
The truth is, everything I see looks like you;
each day feels like a broken game of "I Spy."

I will always want to see and say more to you,
but I feel like I should just say, "goodbye."
And know "good" will come to us both again—
and this time, it'll just say, "hi."

m a r c h

March reminds me
that time is marching on—
and the colors in the trees remind me
that spring is here,
even though you are not
and the earth reminds me
that the flowers don't stop from springing
just because my heart is still in winter

Life doesn't wait for anyone
and neither does death—
both are ready whenever they are ready,
whether we are or not

The world will keep on moving on
even when I haven't—

And the seasons will change
even when I don't want to accept them—

And time is marching on
regardless of if I like it or not—
and it is up to me to choose
whether I will remain halted
or decide to march on with it

Life doesn't wait for anyone
and neither does death--

both are ready
whenever they are ready,
whether we are or not

something new

We used to write on pizza boxes;
now I write alone.
I write on every dying sunset
hoping you'll resurrect inside a poem.
Airplanes climb across this pastel sky,
and I wonder where you could be.
I know you're alive—I know you're free—
but it feels like you've died to me.
I'm mourning the loss of you
while still loving you behind the scenes;
still hoping for your happiness
even though I won't be there to see.
I love you endlessly.
You've been the anchor in my stormy seas;
in waters calm, you've been my peace—
and I'll always keep a piece of you.
Even when this sunset's through,
it'll rise again and I will too—
and every time, I'll think of you.
Knowing that as this night breaks into day,
we'll both *break* into something new.

b o t t l e   c a p s   a n d   s i m p l e r   t i m e s

I have two bottle caps on my windowsill
from our date at the Soda Bar
on a trail by the train tracks
back when our only worries were
what flavor of soda we wanted
and what patch of grass
would hold our picnic blanket
We laid beside the trees
and read each other bad poetry
and laughed and wrote our own
while the screaming steel dwindled into the distance

Everything was perfect then
and it felt good to finally know you
and understand what it means
to share a secret language with someone

But now, we are just two bottle caps,
remnants of two people who were lucky enough
to be alive and in love together
And although we may have not
been designed to stay that way,
I think of you every time I pop bottle caps
and each time I sit down for picnics
but I see you *everywhere*, in everything;
in my own reflection in the mirror, even—
and each time, I muster a smile through the tears,
knowing that my life has been bettered
because *you* were in it

But now, we are just
two bottle caps,
remnants of two people
who were lucky enough to be
alive and in love together

kind, gentle, handsome

I fell in love with a boy
with a poem on his ribcage
and a "be better" tattoo
on his collarbone
and he did just that;
he always was bettering himself—
growing like weeds
except more gracefully,
and blossoming everywhere
His energy was infectious
and it spread to everyone who met him

and I'm sure
it is still spreading—
it's who he is—
kind, gentle, handsome;
with emeralds for eyes
and a heart of gold
I loved him for all of it
and for making me
want to be better too

Be Better.

my perfect memory

I'll always be okay;
I'll stand tall until my end.
But underneath this sturdy smile,
I'm missing my best friend.
My one person that I go to
for every laugh and cry.
The one person that I trust
with every aspect of my life.
I want you to know,
that even though I'll be okay,
the times you cross my mind
are the best parts of my day.
You've given me more love
than I believed I'd ever know;
the tender heart below your chest
has never failed to show.
I always said I'd never have tattoos,
but you're tattooed across my soul,
as my *two-year perfect memory*
who made my broken pieces whole.

these orange walls

These walls are orange and full of warmth—
I suppose they intend to make me feel the same;
the fuzziness, the acceptance, the security inside this box.
And I do feel safe, and welcomed, and hopeful,
and filled with unhinged ambition—
but I also feel blue, and empty, and cold,
and missing a boy,
and missing who I am with him

But I'm learning how to love these walls anyway
How to make friends with myself again—
introduce myself, make my own acquaintance
I'll fall in love with the way
I dance alone with tear-stained cheeks
and with how I fall asleep crying
but wake up and brave the next day with a smile
How sometimes, I drive in complete silence
while other times, I rattle off a novel to God,
hoping He'll take notes for me
I'll fall in love with how I'm not afraid to write alone
at parking garages and at coffee shops
and take myself on lunch dates and night drives
How even when I am empty,
I am never soul-less.
How despite it all, I make it a point to walk outside of
these orange walls, look up at the sky, and be thankful.

walls are orange
full of warmth
suppose they intend
make me feel the same
fuzziness, the acceptance
safeness inside this box
I do feel safe
el secure and hopeful
full of ambition
also blue and empty
old and
g a boy who I am
missing with him
learning how to love those walls anyway
to make friends with myself again
love myself, make my own acquaintance
in love with how
dance alone while
cheeks are tear-soaked
I can find beauty
this sadness
even when my heart is
shredding. I wake up and

how even when I'm
weak I put one foot ahead of
the o
my ability
to lose
and
survive!!

how even when
I'm empty, I'm
never
SOULLESS

how I can
go to bed at
and wake
with
a smile

the reason you smile

Has this been easy for you? Losing me?

You make breathing look easy and I am suffocating without you. I truly want your happiness, but I selfishly hurt thinking you are happier without me. I miss your smile. I miss being the one putting it there.

crescent heart

When I was a kid,
I used to think the moon was cut in slivers
I was always confused when some days
it was round and full
and other days it was just a slice

I had no idea it was whole—
I just thought it was regrowing itself each night;
the way sea crabs regrow their legs
and sand lizards regrow their tails
But not everything grows back so easily

How do I grow my heart back
after I've given it away?
Maybe it's just like the moon;
it was never gone—
it's just been dark here for a while
and a day will come
when the light of life will overtake me
and my crescent heart will become full again

thrifting for love

I have yet to unravel myself—
I have yet to unstitch the reasons why
I continually exchange miles of myself
for millimeters from others.
I desire too little from people.

Perhaps I have spent too much time in thrift stores,
finding beauty in two-dollar jackets
and in thirty-five cent t-shirts.
Perhaps I see too much promise
in hand-me-downs.
Perhaps I have become too accustomed
to sifting through the unwanted.

I'll upcycle them if I need to;
patch them up, hem them down,
fashion them into something
I can see myself wearing.
Perhaps this is the problem.
I'm only looking for reasons to love them
instead of reasons to *not*.

Perhaps I have spent
too much time in thrift stores,
finding beauty in two-dollar jackets
and in thirty-five cent t-shirts.

Perhaps I see too much promise
in hand-me-downs.

b a r r e n

I want to be done with love,
but my heart has so much to give
Even when it's empty,
it wants to give a little more—
pour a little more into a thirsting heart
when mine's already parched,
shriveling from heat waves
of finding false love
and losing real love

I've been wandering in circles
in an endless desert,
stopping to water every cactus
in hopes that they'll bloom
and I'm slowly losing energy
to press forward
and quickly losing hope that
anything lies beyond these hills of sand
to replenish me

reminding myself

At the end of things,
I will find new beginnings,
and beginnings will find you too.

the perfect fit

I'm learning that love has its limits when it is shared with the wrong person. It doesn't mean that they did anything wrong; they just weren't right for you, and that's okay. I'm learning that sometimes you have to let go of people even if you love them. Sometimes, *love isn't enough.*

Why would anyone want to be with someone who wasn't designed specifically for them? It's like jamming two pieces of a puzzle together, knowing they don't fit, but leaving them because they are "close enough." They might look fine together, but they weren't *made* for each other. The colors and shapes will never perfectly align. The big picture will always be a little off. The puzzle will never truly be complete. And you'll always be left wondering what your life would have been like if you had waited for the perfect fit.

I'm learning that sometimes you have to let go of people even if you love them.

Sometimes, love isn't enough.

better apart

Maybe we are not meant to be together.
Maybe you and I are the sun and the moon.
We can only reflect each other—
my midnight is your noon.

Maybe you light up the world from your end,
and I light up the world from mine.
And maybe that's the only way
for each of us to shine.

MAYBE YOU LIGHT UP
THE WORLD FROM YOUR END,

AND I LIGHT UP
THE WORLD FROM MINE.

AND MAYBE THAT'S THE ONLY WAY
FOR EACH OF US TO SHINE.

housekeeping

I've spent too much time
at the wrong doors
in the wrong houses
kissing the wrong faces
and holding the wrong hands—
I've spent too much time in places
I never intended to visit,
and built houses with feeble foundations
knowing they'd never stand—
I've made sandcastles my homes
knowing the tide was coming,
but I stayed there anyway—
until the walls caved in around me
and still, I grasped the sand beneath my fingertips
as the torrents tore me away from it

I've made my heart a hotel room
and given keys to temporary travelers,
hoping one day love would check in
and never leave—
as if love is an *accident*
or coincidence, or happenstance—
and not something that is earned,
and built, and maintained

I've spent too much time treating love like gambling—
carelessly rolling my heart like dice
and *expecting* that one day,
I'd land on something miraculous

I've spent too much time throwing my love away
and placing bets on everyone but myself—

I placed a welcome mat outside my door
before a door was even built—

I've spent too much time house hunting
when I should have been house*keeping*—
pouring cement foundations
and securing sturdy framework—
I should have been building
both front and back porches,
and laying rock gardens and pathways,
and planting bushes for the butterflies,
and hanging sugar water for the hummingbirds—
I should have been installing insulation,
and light fixtures, and hardwood floors,
and choosing cabinets and counter-tops—

And by the time I began decorating,
and manicuring the walls with art,
and stocking the bookshelves with stories,
and filling the vases with freshly-picked flowers,

maybe then, I would have been ready to open the door
and put down the welcome mat
and wait for something *right* to knock

I'VE SPENT TOO MUCH TIME HOUSE HUNTING
WHEN I SHOULD HAVE BEEN HOUSEKEEPING

w a i t i n g

I hope you wait for someone
who loves you like
you give all of the color to the world—
like the earth is a coloring book,
and you are the very thing
that brings this pale blue dot to life.
Like the world is only contour lines,
and emptiness, and shades of gray
without you in it.

And if they look at you
with any less enchantment
than when they look at the sky
on a cloudless day,
or at sunsets when the horizon
bleeds out in shades of red,
then *keep waiting*.

You are meant to be loved
like the world comes to life
when you rise each morning
and like it dies each night
when you close your eyes
and go to sleep.

You are meant to be loved
like the world comes to life
when you rise each morning

and like it dies each night
when you close your eyes
and go to sleep.

PART IV

THE UPHILL CLIMB

It's the most dreaded part of the journey; the uphill climb. The incline that seems it will never reach a plateau. The doubts, the insecurities, the fear that this journey doesn't get easier. It's even harder when you're braving this incline alone. When your eyes sting from your sweat and tears and you can barely see the path ahead of you. When the only thing you are holding onto is the hope that there will be an end to it. A peak with a breathtaking view. When all you can keep doing is pedal one foot ahead of the other and hope that one day, you'll wind up where you need to be.

This section is about the challenging periods, the uphill climbs, of my life. The times where I've been stuck in between sleeping too much and not enough. The times where the air is so thick it feels like I'm drowning in it. The times I've questioned who I am and where my place is in this world. The times in my life when I've felt that everything ahead of me is out of reach. The times I've felt completely isolated, alone, depressed, unworthy, and filled with doubt. The times I've *forgotten to live*. This is about the internal battle within myself; the tug of war between pressing forward and spiraling backwards.

doubts

Doubts seep in with such secrecy,
they are invisible almost;
like polluted water,
I don't notice their presence
until after they've tainted my system,
infested my bloodstream.

Doubts are devious;
showing up like fingerprints on a crime scene
or worms inside an apple—
they often go unseen until the damage is done.

And here I am—
doubt-riddled and bed-ridden—
wondering if I've ever contributed
anything meaningful to the world,
wondering if my life
has ever dared to carry a purpose.

better company

Sometimes the night comes
and brings Sadness with it.
A lot of times, actually.
I scald my skin in shower water,
hoping to scour this ache from my chest,
but instead, it removed a layer of my skin.
I love the hot water though; it calms me.
For a moment, the water and steam
rush against me and I forget
Sadness has ever come to visit at all.

But when I walk out of the bathroom,
it is waiting for me, patiently.
It sits at the foot of the bed
and invites me over.
The day has been long,
and I am tired,
so I oblige to crawl under the sheets
and keep it company.
It isn't the pleasant kind, though.
My heart is heavy.
Sometimes, the pain is unbearable.
Sometimes, I wonder where my place is
in this world I call home.
Wow, I need some better company.

I'm not promised another morning,
but I'm thankful for a chance at it.
Maybe it will bring Happiness along.

SOMETIMES, THE PAIN IS UNBEARABLE
SOMETIMES, I WONDER WHERE MY PLACE IS
IN THIS WORLD I CALL HOME

not today

Am I okay?

That's a question for another day.
Tomorrow I'm busy—
the other days I'll be away—

Am I okay?

Sorry, I can't pick up the phone,
so leave a message at the tone—
but I'll always be a call away.

Just not today.

maybe tomorrow

The birds sing that I will be okay
Maybe tomorrow, not today

a loss of imagination

As a child,
I would lie in the grass
and watch as the clouds
took shape before my eyes—
they wafted through the air, telling stories,
and I felt like I was a part of something

And at night,
I would lie in a bunk bed
and stare at the popcorn ceiling
and watch as ridges formed into faces of people
who became my friends—
and the next night I'd examine the ceiling
until I found their familiar faces
and I watched the adventures unfold again

As a woman,
I wonder if I'm forgetting
to find stories in ceilings
and in the sky—
Instead of paying attention
to the world around me,
I wonder if I've only been walking
with my head down
What if I've only been looking at my feet?
and even then,
I still don't know
what they look like

I wonder if I'm forgetting

to find stories in ceilings

and in the sky

slipping into monotony

I remember days
when just the sight of dandelions
and the carpenter bees
that surrounded them
was enough to fulfill me
I was completely content
with my existence
and with my place in the world
I didn't see myself as small
compared to the vastness of the universe—
instead I saw myself
as a contributing individual,
harmonious with the other creation

Sometimes I wonder
if I have lost that innocence—
I wonder if I've been tainted
by the aches and troubles
that coexist with being human
Have I lost my enchantment
for the simplicities in life?

When the night comes,
do I even notice the fireflies anymore?
or look up to spot the Big Dipper,
or thank the stars for their light?

or do I simply
get out of my car,
and walk into my apartment
without taking even a second
to see anything
except darkness.

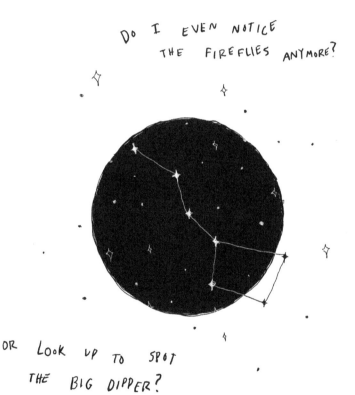

DO I EVEN NOTICE
THE FIREFLIES ANYMORE?

OR LOOK UP TO SPOT
THE BIG DIPPER?

OR THANK THE STARS
FOR THEIR LIGHT?

hidden places

I used to look for things
in hidden places
Like under the stones,
the spaces
held salamanders
and their backs
held colors
that were always exciting
Their orange spines
held black spots
like mini black holes,
like the ones
in the centers of galaxies,
and they vacuumed me into them
just the same

I used to have a mind
that was curious
about everything
and eyes eager
for everything unseen

I used to look for things
in hidden places
but now I look *at* things
in open spaces
Reach for things
already in front of me
Long for things
my eyes have already seen

Or maybe I am
lazier than that—
Maybe I don't reach
for anything
Maybe I sit idly
and wait
for the open spaces
to reach *me*
Wait for the wonders
of the world
to find *me*
For the sights
to see *me*
Maybe I close my eyes
and dream of all
the worlds
I want to visit
and still, I wonder
why *my* world is dark
when I'm the one
whose eyes are shut.

r u s h   h o u r

I don't want to live beneath my eyelids
but I don't know how to wake up—
Even when I am awake,
my eyelids are heavy
from carrying skylines of skyscrapers and sidewalks

It's rush hour
and the streets are congested—
the vehicles are honking and braking
and I can feel every jolt— like bolts of lightning

The people are hurrisome
and bustling and bumping into each other
impatient to escape workplaces
and experience life outside of cubicles
and I can feel every footstep
pounding into my eyelids like elephants—
left, right, left, right, left,
right— I just

           need

               to slee—

i'm just here

Sometimes, I want to run away.
Sometimes, I wish I could catch wind and disappear
into the boundless blue, but I'm here and I don't know
what I'm doing with myself.

hide and seek

There is a gap in my life's timeline—
and I don't know where it began,
but somewhere between 2 and 23
I have misplaced the girl
who loved to dance in the rain.

Now the rain and I play hide and seek,
except I am never seeking—
I am always the one hiding and running away from it
like it will destroy me with one drop—
as if I am not made of it already

There used to be a girl
who looked forward to the rain.
In their game of hide and seek,
she was always the seeker—
and she celebrated finding it by frolicking in it

She was shoe-less and worriless;
her bare feet twirling
as if the earth was her stage
and she was a dancer in life's music box—
overjoyed to be spinning
to the choreography of the clouds
and the rhythm of the rain

But now there is a girl
afraid of getting her hair wet,
and I am trying to find the girl in the gap again

Sometimes I forget to dance in the rain,
I always run from it
like it will destroy me with one drop
as if I am not made of it ~~at~~
~~I am made of of r~~

As a girl I looked forward to it
romped around in it shoeless
my barefeet twirling
the ~~world~~ earth was as if
my stage to my
and the rain was the melody
and I was a dancer
overjoyed to be moving
~~to~~ with the rythyn
of the rain

as if the earth chose her
to be a dancer in life's music

her barefoot twirling in audition

who am i

I wonder if on my journey
to become someone
I'm becoming someone I'm not

harmful state of mind

Why am I so bitter?
I catch myself ripping petals
from the He-loves-me-nots,
tearing heads off of the Black-eyed Susans,
crushing rosebuds beneath my feet

I'm mad at the flowers
for no reason at all
besides that they are beautiful
and I am not

g o d ' s   t i m i n g

All right, I'll write.
All right, I'll write.
Why else am I awake tonight?
I guess God is picking up His hand
and asking me to be the pen this time.
...At this hour.
So all right, I'll write.
I'm not sure what about,
but I'm sure He has a story to tell.
It better be divine.

it better be divine

I've just not been thinking right.
Or too much; it's hard to sleep at night.
And believe me, I'm exhausted,
but I go nowhere when I close my eyes.
Wherever the mind's supposed to go,
mine's been avoiding boarding flights.
Before I know it, the sun is stirring
and waking up the world with light.
The coffee pots are whirring,
the car engines all ignite.
The neighbor's footsteps rouse
the ceiling floor awake,
the birds are chirping with delight.
Everything is beginning to hum in harmony,
but I'm off key, and I still have a flight to catch.

still awake

What else am I supposed to do?
Now that my writing session's through,
I'm still awake.
Maybe I need to take some time to pray.
Maybe you want to talk to me
about the day before it breaks.
And I'm breaking too.
So maybe that's what you're wanting to talk to me about.
Maybe you'll console my doubts.
Maybe you'll fix me or show me how to fix myself.

Maybe you want to talk to me about the day before it breaks.

And I'm breaking too.

r i g h t

So you see,
sometimes I don't write the words;
instead the words write me.
And that's when the writing feels most *right*.

trail of tears

Every day feels like a war to be awake
and every night feels like a war to be asleep.
When the morning comes, I am not ready for it;
I am still wrestling with the night.
When the night comes, I am *still* not ready;
I am fighting with the morning.

I am struggling to find peace
on this trail of tears I'm drowning in.
I don't know how to win
this battle that's already been lost.

in the dying of it all

I came to the parking garage to write; to string together some words and hope that they capture how I'm feeling. But instead, I've been lying on the hood of my car, thinking about life and how I don't know if I feel anything anymore. I feel like I need to cry, unbury my sadness, my frustrations, my exhaustions. But I just lie here, expressionless. Like a carcass in a casket. Staring at the sky. Wondering if I can ever resurrect myself; my happiness. Wondering if everything really does happen for a reason, while knowing deep within that it does. *It has to.* Life is too intricate to be an accident; and mine, too. Something better *has* to be coming. The sun is setting and I'm trying to find good in the dying of it all. I just don't know what that is yet.

Something better has to be coming.

The sun is setting and I'm trying
to find good in the dying of it all.

I just don't know what that is yet.

s e l f - h a t e

I have a magnitude of love
for everyone around me
and not enough for myself.

s t u c k

The sun is awake
and I am also trying to be awake
Sometimes I lie down in bed
and get stuck
like velcro to the mattress
The night comes and goes
but I stay put—
motionless in the whirl
of the morning

I need to move
but I'm embroidered to the sheets
and don't know how to escape—
My body resists every attempt
to unstitch myself
from this fabric I'm woven into

but I lean forward a last time,
seams bursting—
threads tearing in the sunlight—
finally, one of my feet
touches the carpet
and my pin cushion heart
pumps what is left of it
to stay awake
and make it through another day

somewhere in between

I am somewhere between
broken and mending
and beginning and ending;
I am a walking coffee blend,
somewhere between bitter and sweet—
brewed from a dark roast of heartache
and a light roast of love

pumped with night drives and day walks
with an espresso shot
of good music for bad mornings,
a spoonful of sunsets for sad evenings,
and frothed with a smile
and a little art

And to be truthful,
I don't even know my coffee terms—
or the difference between
a latte and a cappuccino—
but basically I'm somewhere
between finding and losing myself
and sometimes the only thing
keeping this walking coffee cup from spilling
is the thought that someone else
might need their caffeine today

I am a walking coffee blend,

brewed from a dark roast of heartache

and a light roast of love

opus 56

It's Opus 56 living in my radio
It's the black keys of the piano
It's the crescendo ascending
It's the windows rolled down
and the wind descending
into my car, my hair—
it's everywhere
It's my sunglasses masking
my tears collapsing
It's losing my Poppa—
It's driving home a last time and knowing it
It's the process of dying and we're all doing it
I just wish it could be me first—
me in your place, lying
Not you, Poppa
Not you, Poppa
Not you, Poppa
It's screaming
It's screaming so loud my lungs hurt
But your lungs are drowning right now, Poppa
The fluid, it's building—
and the piano is too
It's pulling in your driveway
It's walking into your room
It's holding your face
It's the last "I love you's"
It's the black keys fading
It's the music ending
It's you too.

sue

Her life was like a music box, like the one that I cherished as a child; the one that sits atop my dresser drawers, sprinkled with dust, yearning for another chance to be seen and heard. Her heartbeat, her music of life, dwindled slowly, like the end of the familiar tune of that box. I can distinctly remember the hesitant clicking of the crank beneath the box—the slowing of a song that did not want to give up just yet.

Normally, I would get up and rewind the crank until it could not turn anymore and play the tune again. But her melody could only be played once, and I knew that from the day that I met her. I knew that I would have to close my eyes and listen to her song with my undivided soul. I was to embrace each stanza, each note, each beat, and each rest while I had the opportunity. Even with that knowledge, I still could not help but wish that I could play her song again. But I leaned over her bed, one hand in hers and the other on her mattress, my hunched shoulders allowing my ponytail to hang over her body, and submitted to the reality of the situation.

Then, a heartbeat could not be found. The music ended. The box stopped turning. The clicking ceased. A bottomless void assembled. And I was just there, lying at the edge of the abyss, holding her hand tightly so that she would not fall from me into the unknown. But she began slipping from my fingers, her leverage getting the best of me. When I let go of her hand, she fell into that new, and real, black hole.

Her melody could only be played once,
and I knew that
from the day that I met her.

I was to embrace

                          each stanza,

                   each note,

                         each beat,

and each rest

         while I had the opportunity.

o b l i v i o n

Today, I felt desolate.
Today, I felt out of control.
Every now and then,
the gardens within me grow rampant
and I don't know how to stop them.
Today, the loneliness flourished.
I love music, but there was no room
inside for a song to occupy.
I love sunlight, but today I couldn't
find a ray that would brighten me.
I don't know what it is lately.

I feel like a balloon;
I'm filled with so much emptiness,
with one small prick I could rupture—
so I'll choose to avoid everything
and feel nothing.

I'm just floating off into oblivion—
into more empty space.

Every now and then,

the gardens within me grow rampant

and I don't know how to stop them.

Today, the loneliness flourished.

today's storm

I can feel her pain, the earth's—
as thunderstorms fill her sunset eyes,
I wonder who it was
that broke her heart today

It could have been any of us;
I know I have been unpleasant plenty of days.

She grumbles in agony
as her vibrant sky
is clouded with darkness

I feel a silent connection with the earth;
we have never been afraid to show our emotion.

Her tears collapse onto my hair
and I do not run from them
or seek shelter
or rummage for my umbrella

Today, I will be the earth's shoulder to cry on.

r e s i l i e n c e

From the deepest pain
and the darkest hours,
comes the fiercest rain
and the fairest flowers

So when my heart breaks
and my hope cowers,
will these tears awaken
a strength that towers?

e m p t y d a y s

Another empty page again,
another empty day again.
I've always been optimistic,
so it feels wrong to write when I'm not happy—
when I have no more praises left
to come out of my feeble fingertips—
when I have no more reassurance left
to come out of these hapless hands—
I don't want to fill this page with wreckage,
but I'm weather-beaten, worn by living,
and I never knew it could be so exhausting
to place one foot ahead of the other
and one word ahead of the other

I feel sick and can't tell if I'm feverish
or just broken—
I need to find something good to say,
but I've given all my hope away
and I know I'm not hopeless,
just a little hollow right now

But at least I'm being noticed by the wind
and this lowering sun
as they dance along my hair and skin
and soon it will end—
but I will keep living,
and keep filling these pages
with the emptiness, even

another empty page again

another empty day again

I've always been optimistic,

it feels wrong to write

when i'm not happy ~~happy~~

when I have no more praises

of ~~come out~~ to come out of my fingertips — these
hands

when reassurance isn't plenty

hope is empty

don't want to fill this page with

wreckage but i'm weather-beaten.

worn by living

and I never knew it could be so exhausting

to place one foot ahead of the other

and one word ahead of the other

I need to find something good to say

but I've given all my hope away

and I know I'm not hopeless

just a little empty right now

but I'm being noticed by the wind

this lowering sun as they

dance along my hair and skin

and soon it will end

and I will keep living

and fill these pages with ~~even~~ the emptiness ever

consolation

hope

reassurance

dismal

hopeless

when n

reassuran

left to

out

and

tell

fever

jus

brok

here

Even in my emptiness, I am here, taking up space;
hoping to somehow make the world a better place.

knee-deep in comfortability

I'm wading in familiar
and I'm drowning in the skin I'm in.
Change is calling out to me;
it's my time to begin.

jealousy

I am disgusted that she resides in me still
though I've stripped her away from me for years—
I've watched her peel off of me
like dead skin—
I've picked at her,
watched her flake off
like nail polish—
I've ripped her to shreds,
watched her ugly colors
fall to the floor
like aged wallpaper—

Sometimes, I am sure that I have scrubbed my soul
with enough vigor to strip myself of her permanently—
shed her skin from me for the last time—

but layer
        after
                layer,
she slithers her way back—
swelling
        beneath
                the
                        surface—
sinking
        into
                my spirit
with fangs filled with envy—
She broods at everyone's beauty—

She flicks her forked tongue
and convinces me
I should look more like them.
I should change   my hair
widen   my wardrobe
but be myself—
just *different*
She spits in the eyes
of everyone's successes
and hisses all the reasons
they don't   deserve   to see them—
all while asking me,
Why can't you be more like them?

She's a part of me,
but she isn't me.
Maybe one day I'll crucify her—
stab her in the side
only to find that there is
nothing left of her to strain from me

And when she's gone,
I'll resurrect as someone
who celebrates your successes
and finds joy in your jubilee—
I will behold your beauty
while appreciating my own—
I will love you, my sweet neighbors,
without shedding the love I have for myself
because I believe in a world
where we should all uplift each other;
a world where we are all triumphant.

c h a p s t i c k

I have always been my own hype woman.
I have always found something to love about myself
and carried it throughout the day like chapstick—
reapplying when I start to doubt myself

I'm here for myself like the soles of my shoes
that absorb every thump into the ground
and each sharp rock so I don't have to be impaled—
I am my protector.
I show up for myself today, and every day,
when I feel the least important,
and when I feel like a revolving door
for people to walk through me

I am here for myself like I need to be,
but sometimes I need to hear it from someone else—
sometimes I need to feel like
a piece of art hanging on someone's bedroom wall—
I need to know that someone is admiring
the good qualities that I can't see in myself
Sometimes I need someone to
proudly show me off despite my imperfections

Sometimes my chapstick isn't enough
and I need someone else's
when my own words of affirmation are drying out

Sometimes I need to feel
like a piece of art
hanging on someone's bedroom wall

I need to know that someone
is admiring the good qualities
that I can't see in myself

true to myself

I write a lot of sad poems. And I am sad often. But more than that, I am hopeful. I am thankful for the heaviness because I can appreciate the lightness when it comes. On those days, I will fly. Sometimes, I rhyme. Other times, I let the words do what they wish. They can walk wherever they please as long as they tell their story well. Sometimes, I care about everything; other times, I wonder if I've ever found anything to love at all. I have written short poems and long poems. Both have their place. Sometimes, I feel a tug to keep going; other times, I feel at peace with where they are. Some poems are meant to die quicker than others. Of one thing I'm certain; I'm thankful I'm not stuck in one place. I never want to be complacent. I always want to be growing. I always want to move forward. I never want to backtrack, even if I stumble every now and then. I will always stand up and continue pressing on; one foot ahead of the other, one word ahead of the other. Above all, I always want to be vulnerable. I always want to be honest.

And above all, I always want
to be vulnerable, I always want
to be honest.

I write a lot of sad poems.
And I am sad often. But more than that,
I am hopeful. I am thankful for
the heaviness because I can appreciate
lightness when it comes.
Sometimes I rhyme. Sometimes I let the
words do what they wish, they can
long as they tell their stories well
Sometimes I care about everything
and other times I wonder if I've even
found anything to love at all.
I have written short poems and long
poems. Both have their place. Sometimes
I feel a tug to keep going, other
times I feel peace with where they
are at. One thing I am certain of
is I'm thankful I'm not stuck in
one place. I never want to be
complacent. I always want to see
growth. I always want to
move forward. I never want
to backtrack

things i've been
noticing lately

Lately I've been noticing,
I'm always bringing winter's spring.
I'm always here to summon warmth
to hearts grown cold with frigid sting.

I turn gray skies to blue,
so no one thinks that I get blue—
it's like they've forgotten I'm a human,
with more emotions than I know to do with;
and I've got no one to spew them to—
or at least that's how it feels sometimes—
who knows if it's the truth.

But lately I've been noticing,
I'll light the paths before their feet
and I'll let the shadows fall on me,
if it only means that they can see.
And this is who I want to be—
be there for anyone in need—
but often times, I'm just
a stepping stone in someone's dreams
and when they find out where they're going,
their destination isn't me.
So it feels like their life's been on a lock,
and I am just the key.

So I'm here for myself at the end of the day;
I've had to adapt to be this way.
I need validation too,
but *I'll* have to be the one to say,
that regardless of what life has in store,

I'll always be okay.
I'll always choose to see the rainbow's bend
even when I'm dripping, drenched in rain.
I'll always look up to admire the stars
and learn them all by name.
And I'll know that Someone's looking down
and wants to know me just the same.

And knowing this is comforting;
because lately I've been noticing
that no one seems to notice me.

Notice me.

Lately I've been noticing,
    I'm always bringing winter spring
    i'm always here to summon warmth
    to hearts grown cold with frigid sting.
    I turn grey skies to blue,
    so noone thinks that I get blue
    ~~as~~ like they've forgotten I'm a human
    with more emotions than I know to do with
And I ~~am~~ have ~~but~~ noone to spew them to
as least that's how it feels that way ~~feels~~ sometimes,
    who knows if it's the truth.

ately I've been noticing
ight the paths before their feet,
    i'll let
nadows   Lately   I've been noticing,
on me   that   no one   seems   to
    only means   (notice   me)
++   they can see.

    But often times ~~the~~ only ~~best~~
    I'm just a   stepping stone
    (in someone's ~~close~~ dreams,

nd when they find out where they're going
eir destination ~~is without some~~ ✗ isn't ne
~~is without some~~ is without

for myself
af the
of
da

I'
had to

vali-
Sometimes,

I'll
have
be.
one

and
this
is who
want tha
be
for
in

that regardless of what life has in store,
I'll ~~ta~~ always be okay,
I'll always ~~chose to~~ see the rainbow
even when I'm ~~blinded by~~ drenched in
I'll always ~~step the~~ notice stars
and ~~know~~ them by ~~your~~ name
~~Just the~~ And remember all by
~~That someone~~ that we are
all the same
~~and know that~~
and someone's looking down on
me and I doing the same
Someone is looking
down and wants
to know me just the same

And knowing that is comforting
because lately I've been noticing
that no one seems to
notice me.

h i g h   t i d e

I will not apologize for my feelings;
I cannot help that my heart is like the moon
pulling tidal waves out of my tear ducts
whenever it pleases

It's high tide
and I will not apologize
for my eyes carrying oceans—
I cannot control the currents
that crash against the coastlines of my cheeks
and seep into my pores
and the shores of my lips

I am not meant to pretend
that I am never wavering
or tossed with life's wind—
I am not meant to pretend
that I am always tip-toeing in the shallow end
when hurricanes and tsunamis
are building and billowing within

I am not meant to be steel-faced and unphased;
I have never believed that strength
means standing immobile—
like rock cliffs and monuments
and all things towering and unshakable
I believe that strength is remaining soft
even though hardships can easily harden

I believe that strength comes from
honesty and vulnerability—
and from being willing to look at you in the eyes
even though I can barely see
over the waves rising
and capsizing onto my cheeks and chin

and I will not apologize for my voice shaking
over the sound of all of the storms swelling within me
because *I am not ruled by these riptides*
and I will not apologize for choosing to speak
when the high tides could have silenced me

I CANNOT HELP THAT
MY HEART IS LIKE THE MOON

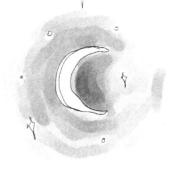

PULLING TIDAL WAVES OUT OF
MY TEAR DUCTS
WHENEVER IT PLEASES

I AM NOT MEANT TO PRETEND
THAT I AM NEVER WAVERING
OR TOSSED WITH LIFE'S WIND

IT'S HIGH TIDE
AND I WILL NOT APOLOGIZE
FOR MY EYES CARRYING OCEANS

I CANNOT CONTROL THE CURRENTS
THAT CRASH AGAINST THE COASTLINES OF MY CHEEKS

new creature

The leaves, they are falling
from the trees like snow;
and snow, it will soon follow—
a sign that things are still changing
in a world where I've become desperately still
The winter is coming,
but it feels like I've been in it since last year—
I never left.

I don't know what it is like to bloom;
how could I when I lock myself away
from all things that resemble sunlight?
The seasons are changing,
and I know I should too—
like a butterfly in need of its wings,
I need to experience the world as a new creature.
I've lived in darkness so long,
I'm not sure I remember what light looks like.
But the cocoon can only contain the caterpillar
for so long before it thrusts itself into the unknown;
it cannot be stopped.

The leaves, they are falling
from the trees like snow,
and the monarchs, they are rising
above the world below,
and I— I too am ridding myself
of the weight I've been holding;

I want to know what it means to live with wings.

We fear change, we settle
for fear of loss and
we lack faith that uncertainty
will bring new beginnings.
So we remain in a stagnant
comfortability. A dull happiness.
The cocoon can only contain
the caterpillar for so long
before it thrusts itself into
unknown ; it cannot be stopped.
the sky pleads to be noticed and
flown in.

afterward, hangs upside down,
flaps wings to straighten and
dry them

wes +
wrinkled

faith of
a butterfly
that the
other side
of familiar
brings
someth
more
than
what

and hope
for future

- wings are wet when it emerges
- heavy but still begin the
- process of change regardless
  of their entrapment
- takes time for them to
  dry and be ready to fly but
  it doesn't stop them from emerging

due to tight
chrysalis
caterpillar is
phasing

w a l t e r h i l l   d a m

I sat below the waterfall
at the dam today.
Sometimes I get so lost
in the routine of living
I forget to stop.
I don't often remember to be.

Oh, but the world is so divine when it is still.

A green heron
sat proudly on top
of the dam's waterfall,
scouring the unfolding water
for minnows.

But I didn't notice him at first,
because he sat so still;
his eyes fixated on the billowing water.
But then he looked up,
his gaze transcending into the distance
and his chest feathers puffed and splendorous.
At this moment,
this was *his* waterfall
and he was the only heron in the world.
The waterfall was bold, loud;
the center of attention, certainly,
and yet the heron
didn't seem to feel small in comparison.
He appreciated it for what it was;
it was his hunting ground after all.

Some leaves rustled behind me
and I jumped.
When did I become so antsy?
I can't even be peaceful when I try.

When I turned back to see the heron again,
he was gone.

My disappointment left
when I noticed he had made his way
down the waterfall and into the stream,
happily waving a minnow back and forth
in his beak; flaunting his prized catch.

I smiled at this;
I haven't seen something so remarkable in a while.
But I want to notice all of it;
everywhere, every day.
I want to be in tune with
this world I'm living in,
but so many times
it feels like life is an instrument
and I am just a broken string
or a faulty key.

Sometimes I feel so separate;
but today, the waterfall was singing
and the heron was melodious
and I am learning to be
a part of this harmonious whole.

PART V

THE DOWNHILL COAST

This is it. This is what the struggle was for. Tears of joy replace my tears of grief as the ground begins to level beneath me and I can finally let go of the pedals. I've made it to the plateau and I can't stop grinning at the sunset. I let the last rays of the day climb all over me like children on monkey bars for the first time. The orange light reflects against my bicycle's surface and I begin reflecting on the journey that led me here.

In this light, I can see everything clearly. I look at my bicycle and can see every nick in the metal, every scrape etched into the paint. The basket, too, is weathered and frayed—but I couldn't love it any more than I do at this moment. It was these battle scars that carried me to the top of this mountain. I can look back on each of these scuffs and remember every fall. There is a story behind each of these imperfections on this bike. Without these stories, I don't think this view would have been as breathtaking. After roads of ups and downs, I have found a balance. My faint feet and weary legs can rest. My heart can be at peace. My soul can cling onto freedom.

I am looking forward to the rest of my ride. It is a downhill coast from here. I'm going to let my feet dangle off of the pedals for a bit and simply admire this world around me.

I'm going to let myself fall in love with this earth again; with this life again. I'm going to wave at every stranger I pass, chirp at every bird that sings to me, and let the cool breeze waltz against my cheeks and eyelashes like I did when I first began. Scars and all, and I am alive and I am grateful, and I'm ready to linger in every moment of this ride home.

new beginnings

We all will encounter
moments of self-doubt—

We will hold loneliness by its hand
and dance on its toes
We will stare at the ceiling
unnecessarily for hours
before finally falling asleep,
if sleeping at all
We will clothe ourselves in sadness
and we will feel its weight
bearing down upon our shoulders

We may spend days, weeks, years even,
yearning for a break-through
But one day,
we will release the loneliness
from between our fingertips
and we will slip off the heaviness
as gracefully as the trees
shed their foliage
on a colorful autumn day

and instead of mourning what we've lost,
we will rejoice for all the space we've created
to allow something more beautiful to take its place

and that isn't to say
that we won't still feel the harshness
of a brisk winter—
we were never promised a life
without suffering.

But one day,
a bud will spring forth to remind us
what it feels like to flourish
and even the sun herself
will envy our light

s h e

She feels it— everything— and feels it with ferocity. Her spirit won't let her do otherwise. She is so willing to love, so willing to give, so willing to connect. But she's unwilling to settle, unwilling to be merely comfortable, unwilling to linger in love with the person who is *almost right*. She hurts, she aches, she is exhausted. But she trusts, she lets go, she moves forward. She endures. She lets loose of what doesn't nourish her and clings onto life, holding fast to the one thing she can depend on to maneuver through this dark and angry world.

She looks for light. She becomes it. *She.*

* landfill ~ clings onto life, ~~like~~ ~~for~~ ~~for dear life~~
    * holding fast ~~because it~~ bec ~~ber~~
    ~~holds~~. hanging onto to hope
                  it all   with ferocity.

She feels it; everything, and ~~feels everything strongly~~.
Her spirit won't let her do otherwise.
She is so willing to love, so willing to give,
so willing to connect. ~~She can~~

~~She~~ But she's unwilling to settle, unwilling
  to merely be comfortable, unwilling to
  linger in love with the person who is almost
  right.
She hurts, she hurts, she hurts, but
She trusts, she lets go, she moves forward.

She endures. She turns everything loose that
doesn't ~~tell her~~ nourish her and
clings onto life, holding fast to the one thing
she can depend on to maneuver through
this dark and angry world.

She looks for light. She becomes it. She.

a morning prayer

My day begins with "rrRrRrrrrRr";
it's the coffee maker's good morning growl
and I am awake and thankful again.
I'm ready to close my eyes and take in the morning.

Thank you God for this opportunity
to soak in your air.
Thank you for the people around me
and the endless love we share.

Thank you for these fingers,
for the chance to create, write, and type.
Thank you for these hands.
Thank you for these eyes.

Thank you for these ears
and for the music they entertain.
Thank you for making this heart
able to withstand so much pain.

You make life bearable
when it is unbearable.
You give me new and promising days.
Thank you for your wondrous ways.

I am ready to begin this day.

gather up your limbs

If you're feeling empty today, gather up your limbs.
Take them on a walk. Drink in the sunlight; fill your
lungs with new air. Let the birdsongs inspire you.
How they lift their heads and sing despite everything.

Inhale the beauty of living. Exhale the rest.

rejuvenation

As time journeys on,
I continue to meet myself over and over again—
learning what I love and don't love,
discovering new things about myself daily.
I am always "me," but am ever-changing—
growing into myself with each season
shedding parts of myself and rejuvenating
losing myself and finding myself again.
I have embarked on this voyage of living and dying
and I will always choose to live.
I will always focus on renewing myself
even after moments of losing everything.

They are only moments.
We can always begin again.

I have embarked
on this voyage
of living and dying
and I will always
choose to live.

a different kind of isolation

Is the world empty
or just full of empty people?

I'm always smiling at everyone I pass by,
and one day they all stopped smiling back.

I didn't know that joy could be so isolating,
but I'm learning more and more each day
that happiness is rejected by most people I meet.
I'm learning that having a cheerful heart
is a lonelier life than I once imagined.
But I'd rather be lonely and joyful
than keep the company of misery.

I could let this all discourage me,
but it is not in my character
to contain my excitement for life
and so I won't.

I still have hopes to find someone
wide-eyed and whimsical, and with a welcoming grin—
and just maybe, they'll smile first.

unshakable

If we don't pay attention,
we can become bitter.
We can unknowingly
become the world's sculpture;
let it chip away at our sweetness,
sand away our joyfulness
mold us with its wry fingers
and leave us to harden
into an image
that looks like hatred
and nothing like
who we were before,
back when we were unshakable
and jovial
and would stop to smell garden lilies
and dared to leave love letters
on windshields
when our daily missions
were to make the ones
around us beam with bliss
If we don't pay attention,
we might stop,
and I don't want to know
that version of myself.

lost and found

The day fills me with life
and the night pours it out of me—

The day hands me hope
and the night trades it for doubt—

The day gives me purpose
and the night steals it away from me—

but I chase after them,
not surrendering
until the day returns all of the things
I've lost in the night
and I have found myself again

The day fills me
~~up wit~~ with life
and the night
pulls it back out of
me
The day fills me
with hope
and the night
replaces it with
        doubt

The day ~~reminds~~
~~me~~ gives me purpose
and the night steals
it and ~~sometimes~~
I chase after it
~~but~~ sometimes I chase
after it ~~but~~
~~ea~~ and catch it

and other times the
morning comes
and I ~~am still~~
haven't found it yet
but I will continue
to run after ~~the sta~~
it   and hope the
~~sun~~ day fills
    me back up

returns with all
of the things he lost
and found

Lost and found

clarity

I thought maybe the sea would speak to me. I thought
that somewhere between the sandy hair and salty skin, I'd
hear something. I sat by the ocean and waited for a clarity
that didn't come. It was just one wave crashing after the
other. Not answers. Or reasons why. The tide just kept
falling against the shore. It couldn't stop if it wanted to.
I guess life keeps on going whether our questions are
answered or not. The only thing we can do is keep living.

g e n t l e   r e m i n d e r s

I am reminded
that I am not alone
in the gentlest of ways—

by the grasshopper latching itself
onto my bicycle basket—

by the monarch tap-dancing
against my shoulder—

by the leaves confusing my hair
with the ground—

by soft smiles,
those sweet gifts given to me by strangers—

Sometimes, I just need to be reminded
that there are still things that notice me
amongst the loneliness of existing

a dance with freedom

In this moment,
she became one with the world around her.
She frolicked along the shoreline
and the waves nervously brushed against her ankles,
asking her if they "could please have this dance."
She twirled in agreement.
The waves crashed in response.
Suddenly, life began to sync up.
Suddenly, she didn't have to think anymore.
She was just a girl spinning
on a billion grains of sand— and that's all that mattered.
It didn't matter what anyone thought of her.
It didn't matter what she thought of herself.
It didn't matter that she was broken.
Or that we all are broken.
We will always be a little broken somewhere.
For a moment, she forgot all of it.

When the tide pulled back, her worries left with it.
They couldn't stay if they wanted to.
She curtsied.
The ocean bowed.
The sky applauded.
In this moment, she was free.

m a g g i e

She is music in a quiet world, a waltz in a still room, a melody gracing the ears of the deaf, even.

let it be

If I am to be caged, let it be in happiness.
If I am to be surrounded, let it be by love.
If I am to be free, let it be from hatred.

If it doesn't uplift me, I'll *let it be*.

my affair with today

I am wildly in love with possibility
and probably too infatuated with tomorrow—

but in my affair with today,
I will hold hope by the fingertips
and dance on the toes of the miraculous—
I will spin freely beneath the arms of purpose,
and mystery, and wonder—
forever finding music in the mundane
and seeing beauty in the most bland of places—

and knowing no destination
as long as love is my loyal companion
on this joyous journey of living

30 things you should never forget about yourself

You are beautiful.

And it's a possibility that no one has ever said those words to you before. Or maybe someone reminds you of how beautiful you are every day. Whether someone else recognizes your beauty or not, maybe you still need to see it for yourself.

So, stand up. Right now, wherever you are, stop whatever you are doing and simply stand up. Walk to the closest mirror, take a deep breath, and look at yourself. Take some time to genuinely look at yourself and think:

I am beautiful.
Even when I feel ugliest, I am beautiful.
Some days, every person I see is a reminder of the person I am not, and I am left feeling empty.
But even at my emptiest, *I am enough.*

I am radiant.
The sun rises each morning to compete with my light.
And on days when darkness consumes me,
I *am* a lighthouse.
I pierce through the darkness.
I am a light and I am destined to be seen.
I am destined to be loved.
I am destined to be cherished.

I cannot make everyone happy; I am only a person.
But I am a great person, and I deserve happiness.
I deserve the kind of happiness
that you hear about in fairy tales—
the kind of happiness that you read about in books,
but question if it truly exists.
I believe that it does.

I will meet sadness in my lifetime, we all will.
But it is up to me to continue walking
until I meet happiness;
and there, *I will choose to stay.*

I am breathing.
I am *meant* to be here because I have been given life
and I am breathing.
I am meant to take up space.
I have a purpose.
I am capable of moving mountains.
I am capable of generating a mere thought into existence.
I *can* make a difference.

Today, I woke up with another breath.
Today, I woke up with another chance to be the person
I have always wanted to be.
Today, I woke up beautiful; *and I will never forget it.*

even after destruction

Plague me.
Place me onto an angry ocean
as a small sailboat
and rip my sails in the tempest.
Engulf me in waves.
Toss me into a handful of lightning.
Drown me beneath the fingertip of a tsunami.
Empty me of all my precious cargo.
Raid me of everything you think I am
and I will continue to be more than that.
Even when you believe I am shipwrecked,
I will show up,
proudly strewn across the ocean floor,
amongst the coral and seaweed and all things colorful
as a beautiful disaster;
a treasure to be explored and sought after
even after destruction.

light-bearer

I want to be a light-bearer.
I want to be the type of person
who ignites fires in people—
even in the people
who think they are
too damp to catch flame,
too empty to generate warmth

If I could,
I would cremate all of your doubts
and bury their ashes
in the deepest parts of the earth
that way you'd never
be hindered by them again.

If I could,
I would show you
that *you* are a light-bearer, too.

the capacity
to be courageous

It is more than easy
to remain where you are comfortable—
to stay where you are at
when the streetlamp is familiar
and the sidewalk has been trodden.

But somewhere
amidst your enslavement
to your fears and doubts
and the uncertainties of tomorrow,
I hope you feel
an immeasurable strength
emerge within you,
along with the capacity to be courageous—
the *willingness* to make the decision
that is not easy.

I hope you feel
an immeasurable strength
emerge within you

relentlessly alive

I once knew someone
brimming with thought.
Their bedside blinds
could not stop the morning sun
from filtering in and flooding their mind with ideas

They were full of imagination
and relentlessly alive from the moment they woke—
and yet they felt farthest from alive
than anyone I'd ever met.
I could never understand
how their thoughts spiraled into darkness
when they themselves were so bright and vivacious

It's strange how the people
who are the most full of life
are actually empty.

What does it take to fill someone up again?
I don't know.
But I'm thankful the sun is shining again this morning.

It's strange how the people who are the most full of life are actually empty.

untitled

I didn't give this a title because when I started writing it, I had no idea of where it was going or what its destination would look like; but then, I realized that this is simply the theme of life. As I have grown and matured, I have realized that worrying about where I am going does nothing but withdraw from my happiness and give me aimless anxieties. So I vow to live each day with eager spirits and in the moment.

This doesn't mean that sometimes I won't slip into doubt about where I am going or who I will become, because being of human nature, I will. But above being human, I am the creation of a perfect Creator, and I am choosing to embrace this journey while knowing that my Creator has a purpose for me more magnificent than I could fathom— *and that itself invigorates me*; knowing that I cannot imagine the intricate ways in which I was designed to change the world around me; the paths I was meant to interweave in this wonderful entanglement of life.

prisoner of jesus

I'm a prisoner of Jesus;
I'll never be the same.
I've taken on his name for evermore.
I've tried to run and hide,
but I just can't get away.
I'm a prisoner of Jesus,
and that's the way I'll stay.

h o p e

I know it's there, it's in the air—
Hope; it's hard to find when life strips us bare
But I'll search for it on the wings of a prayer;
I know eventually it will come back to me.
One day hope won't be hard to see.
My hardened heart will soon be free.
I know it's there, *it's in the air*.

house hunting

In our endeavor for acceptance of our bodies,
we have crafted a casual hookup culture.
Our bodies have become welcoming carcasses
for others to be the vultures.
We are feasted on and ravaged
and left with nothing but our bones.
Temporary rather than permanent,
we allow people to come and go—
and yet we wonder why we are seen
as only a house instead of *home*.

But I refuse to be seen for only my body
and the pleasure it can give,
and I choose to be seen for only my heart
and the *treasure* it can give.
I refuse to be reduced
to a number on a man's list
of women whose clothes he's stripped.
I refuse to be just a name he'll forget
once another woman has his taste on her lips.
I won't become a number in his body count
of women he'll forget about—
so don't come to me
if you're only looking for a house.

Until I'm wanted as a home,
I'll choose to live without.

this miracle of living

I want to immerse myself
in the world around me
Forget routines,
the mundane cycle
of only existing
I want to be an emulsion
in this wonderful dispersion of life;
An anther in the lilies,
a lullaby of the whippoorwill,
a crest in an unfolding wave,
the last breath of a dying star,
I want to experience it all—

It is not enough for me
to only see it,
this miracle of living—
I don't want the world
to pass me by
because I chose to be still
while everything else was
moving in tandem

When I wake,
and the sun tiptoes across my eyelids,
I hope I am overtaken by
an immense and childlike joy
along with an abundant eagerness
to thrust myself into the day
as if it was my first time seeing

I don't want the world
to pass me by because
I chose to be still
while everything else
was moving in tandem

architect of the unwritten

I have an irresistible urge to write—
my body and mind
would rupture
if was not able
to release these words—
these phrases—
these utterances—
like wildfires,
they consume me

The back of my mind
is continually churning,
occupied by crafting sentences
and rearranging phrases;
I tear sentences apart
just to build them back up again

I am an architect of the unwritten—
of what could be—
of turning a thought into something tangible
something that makes me feel alive

c r e a t o r s

I think we are all destined to create.

I think somewhere in each of us
resides a seed waiting to take root
and spread like wild kudzu
swallowing entire towns—

like telephone lines
spanning entire worlds—

like brilliant stars,
those twinkling grains of salt
peppering the entire universe—

I dream of creating overtaking me the same;
with ideas gripping me like tentacles
so I can no longer function
until I turn them into something tangible—
so I can no longer live
until I breathe life into the lifeless

the ultimate artist

Some days, like today, when soaking in the blue sky, bluebirds, and bliss, I begin to drift into the clouds and get lost there. Is there a way to describe them that hasn't been said already? So many people have tried. Many have done so successfully. Sometimes it's hard to believe that there is room for one more voice. It's hard to believe that someone could even offer up a new perspective. Will I say anything different from the next person, or the people before me? We are all living the same life, after all— just differently, and in our own time. I can hear people laughing through my headphones, but it doesn't distract me. I'm still lost in the clouds.

The cloud above me is in the perfect shape of a heart— *I wonder is if this is God's way of letting me know he sees me.* Or maybe it isn't for meant for me at all—but I'm looking, so I can only go by what I'm given. Maybe looking up is my way of showing God that I see him. Either way, I'm lost in his wonder. He's the ultimate artist; can it really be true that I'm his apprentice? I have so much to learn from him and I am watching and observing.

When I see the clouds, all I can do is imagine God finger-painting. He doesn't think too much about it, he just lets his fingers slide across the atmospheric canvas and creates. He gets lost in it. He makes a perfect mess. For the fluffy clouds, he is generous. He isn't afraid to pile on the paint and dab it all over the canvas.

For the feathery ones, I imagine his fingers sweeping across the canvas, so freely, so tenderly, and with much ease. Maybe the angels are singing and he simply allows his hands to follow wherever their harmonies take them. When the clouds take shape, into hearts and dolphins and bicycles; well, I'd like to think that's God's way of showing his sense of humor. I wonder if he stops to see who is looking up and watching his painting session and he drops a little gift right where they are gazing.

And when the clouds move, I imagine them moving from his breath. Surely his breath is that powerful. Sometimes I test his greatness—I ask him to spell out words in the sky if he hears me. But why should he have to prove this to me?

Isn't looking up enough?

breathing for yourself

Selfless darling,
you cannot always
lend everyone your oxygen—
deflate your lungs
from all the giving—
deprive yourself
of your own air—

Sometimes, you have to breathe for yourself;

Plug the faucets—
Clog the gutters—
Throw away the funnels you use
to sift from yourself for others—
Learn not to drain yourself
to see others full—
You congest yourself to set others free;
to allow their air to circulate—
an outpouring of life

Don't you think you deserve that too?

Sometimes, you have to breathe for yourself:

Plug the faucets

Clog the gutters

Throw away the funnels you use
to sift from yourself for others

the aroma of life

I don't know what
it is I'm smelling
on this lovely walk;
I have never been good
at naming the trees and the grasses
like my father is

It must be life—
the eagerness to exist freely
and linger long in happiness

w h i s p e r s   f r o m   g o d

Sometimes it can be difficult to hear God's voice
amongst the noise of existing.
Every now and then I have to separate myself
from the world and lean into the quiet moments.
It is then that I can hear Him everywhere,
and with such clarity.

Take the flowers, for instance;
they are whispers from God reminding us
that even storms are here for us to bloom.

w i n g s

I don't know where I'm walking,
but I hope it is in the right direction.

The air has been colder
and the trees are bare,
making it easy to see
the birds' nests resting comfortably
in the arms of the white oak.

I guess I wanted to
live like the birds today,
because I found my own tree to sit in,
although much smaller
and not near as high off the ground,
as I am bound to my legs and gravity.

I think I will come to this tree more often—
to write and wonder, and give wings to words
I think should take flight.

Maybe they will teach me something.

I walked past places I've lived before
~~before~~ I've picnic tables I've sat in
wondered who I was then
remember being in those moments
not what I was thinking about
what exactly was going on in my life.
is times like these that I wish I
t journals, so I could see snippets
who I was.

much smaller
as I'm ba
to ni
and
g

don't know where I'm walking bot
hope it's in the right direction.

trees are bare, making it easy to
the bird's nests. resting comfortably
the arms of the _____.

guess I wanted to live like the birds
day, because I found my own that
sit in, although much less tall
convince myself that I have limitations

dream-doer

She gave wings to her dreams
and made her wishes take flight
And when the world met her with darkness,
she simply said, "Let there be light."

i need to close my eyes more

Tonight I sat in stillness
and let the night sky envelope me like a warm cloak;
I draped my eyelids shut
and the longer I left them there,
the more the stars swaddled me—the grasses, too—
the scent of the earth—
they all began to greet me.
The sounds, especially,
began to swarm together in symphonies;
the crickets and katy-dids *like mini violas*—
the owls *like trumpets*—
the whippoorwills and nighthawks *like flutes*—

I was overwhelmed by their serenading,
but realized they had never stopped.
They'd crooned their tunes nightly for me;
I just stopped paying attention.

Life is so quiet when we stop listening.
I need to close my eyes more.

a wink in time

When I am with the trees,
I always find myself admiring
some wonderful little creation
and wondering what it would be like
to live more like it.
One day it is the flowers,
the next day it is the birds—
today it is the Mayflies.
I watched them fly along the riverbed and became curious.
The female Mayfly's lifespan is about five minutes.
What an inspiration—
we've all been thrusted into this world
and in a moment we are being thrusted out of it.
I'm not promised more than a Mayfly.
I'm not promised more than a short flutter in the wind.

What am I going to do to cherish
this extraordinary and temporary life?
If I'm only a blink in time,
I hope to at least make it a wink.

If I'm only a blink in time,

I hope to at least make it a wink.

things i want to be

I want to be brave and wince at nothing.
I want to carry love and laughter with me daily.
I want to be filled with goodness and give it freely.
I want to scatter kindness on every sidewalk
and leave smiles on every stranger.
I want to be more alive than possible.
I want to be unpredictable and spontaneous.
I want to be honest and vulnerable.
I want to walk with a spring in my step
and with joy in my heart.
I want to scream when I wish to,
cry when I have to,
and burst with joy when it can't be contained any longer.
I want to live as if *nothing* can stop me
from sharing this story I have to tell.

for you

You do not always have to be running, or doing— or worrying, especially. Some moments are best spent in stillness. Some moments are meant only for breathing, for entering that realm where the only sounds are the gentle breeze of your inhales and exhales along with the pulsing tide of your heartbeats.

Some moments are meant only for you.

u n r u l e d

I always choose journals with unruled paper. My mind doesn't exist between the lines; it clings to the open spaces, but really doesn't cling to any space at all—it gallivants wherever it pleases—dancing freely, and clumsily, and often off-beat. It has plenty of missteps. Sometimes I wish I could reel it in, but I'm learning that I'm destined for open spaces and the ability to wander in any direction without worrying about bumping into anything— this is the only way I know to live and create.

I always choose journals with ~~unruled~~ unruled
my mind doesn't ~~exist~~ exist between the lines
it clings to the open spaces but
really doesn't drg to ~~escape~~ away
space at all —

quite scattered moves freeflowing

and sometimes I
want to reel it in but I
think I'm ~~so~~ just destined
for open spaces and the ability
to wander aimlessly and in
any direction without feeling
like I am going to bump into
anything — this is the
only way I know to
live and create ~~things~~
~~worth meaning~~

*   ~~Re.~~ things worth
                meaning

love to share

Today, I will be rooted in love.
I'll let it seep into my soul and spread freely.
I want love to inhabit every home in my body.
After that, I hope it opens doors for others to enter in.
Shake off your feet,
leave any hatred on the welcome mat.
Step into this heart of mine.
We have love to share.

I want love
to inhabit
every home
in my body.

u n b r i d l e d

I have an excitement for life
that can't be bottled up—
or caged, or stored in a locket

My soul is a flame that cannot be snuffed out,
a treasure that cannot be stolen,
a gift that cannot be returned or exchanged

I want to live like every room
has disco balls on the ceiling
and walk like every floor
is a trampoline beneath my feet—
always dancing,
always keeping a spring in my step—
always searching for another spirit
to share a moment and a laugh with

I will never stop smiling at strangers
and scream-singing at stop signs
and stammering at sunsets—

and I will never put a saddle
on this wild-horse soul of mine—
this untameable excitement
and unbreakable love for living

My soul is a flame
that cannot be
snuffed out
a force that cannot
be stolen
a gift that cannot
be returned or
exchanged or

this excitement is
endless

My soul is free,
it is not my

Souls

lessons from a man
in a thrift shop

I am always meeting people and learning how to live from them. Today's lessons were from an 85-year-old quirky man in a thrift shop. He was so filled with joy, I swore he could burst at any minute. He said two things:

1. You have to learn to give before you can learn to live.
2. If you make someone happy, it makes life worth living.

And after that? He sang. And sang loudly. His voice echoed throughout the store. He didn't stop to think, he just lifted his voice to the heavens without a worry or care. Three shoppers stopped to sing with him. We all felt alive. His soul was free and we all knew it. And I knew it would be an injustice if I didn't pass along his lessons. I hope he makes you smile the way he did me.

this chance at living

I don't know why I am here;
I've just been placed on this earth
without a choice in the matter.

But I will tell you, I love life;
these wonderful breaths I'm taking.
The trees beg me to drink in their earthy exhales
so I can breathe out and replenish them again.
I inhale larger than ever.
"I love this life!"
I scream to the trees, and the birds, and the sky,
and they echo back to me;
the leaves waving in the wind,
the chickadees singing joyously,
the sky grinning bright—
all of them exclaiming,
"We love this life!"
I smile and continue marveling
at the wonders of existing.
At this chance for loving.
This chance for creating.
This chance to be anyone I want to be—
to roam anywhere my feet choose to wander.

meek reminders

I am not here to say that love
just stumbles upon us like in the fairy tales
or that it bumps into everyone at all—
or that life is all gardens and blooming
when it is often weeds and thorns and drought—
and most things die and disappear in winter.
I am not here to say that life is painless and easy
when living is anything but simple—
and with each second we are also dying

Sometimes the sun setting
is the only thing keeping us going—
Sometimes the end of the day
is the only thing giving us the strength
to greet another one—

I am not here to promise anything—
or say that we aren't sometimes broken,
or that we aren't always flawed—
but I am here to say that our brokenness
does not have to break us completely—
and our flaws do not have to be failures—
but meek reminders that we are still here,
daring to face another sunrise—
daring to let the morning light up
these exquisitely imperfect faces
of these fabulously flawed people
in this magnificently troubled—
but *terribly grand world*

wings in a windowsill

When I was a young girl,
and all things were bright and beautiful,
my Nana would pick up the dead butterflies
from her flower gardens and keep them
on the leaves of the plants in her windowsills—
and I would always stop to
wonder at their wings—
and with every visit,
they were still as striped and yellow
as when God first made them

And when I left the windowsill,
I would keep thinking of the butterflies
and of all the ways I'd want to be remembered—
If I could only brighten someone's day
without having to even be there—

My life doesn't have to be magnificent,
or long, or remarkable,
as long as it is meaningful.
I could leave this world
carrying a basket of contentment
if I only knew I had touched someone—
if I knew that one person, even—
was holding onto me like wings in a windowsill,
bringing color to their world
even after death

pocketful of faith

I remember the taste of it,
life before I knew things—
and the void was pleasant,
not made of dark matters
like *too many questions,*
and *too little answers,*
or maybe, *too many tightly-bound answers,*
and not near enough time
to unlace them all

I remember reaching for the sun
before fretting became my fertilizer,
growing me in all of the wrong places
and weeding me of all the right ones
and of the light things I wished to keep

And faith, I've always had it,
and still, I keep it close to me—
though I used to wear it like
puffed sleeves and red lipstick—
but now I keep it tucked away
inside front pockets—
still close to my heart,
but sometimes, I forget I have it there

It is easy to lose sight of faith
amidst the traffic of knowing—
the more I know,
the less I am certain about *anything*

But when my mind begins to wonder,
and wander again with worry—
and my heart begins again to pound,
quickened by the unknown, and doubts,
and all of the dark things rippling within me,

I can feel faith resting here,
a faint force inside my front pocket—
steadily and peacefully
reminding me that it has nothing to do with seeing
or understanding—
and everything to do with feeling
and surrendering—
and knowing that I will never *know* everything
and besides, I can't imagine life being interesting,
or meaningful, or purposeful if I did—
I have always loved to learn, and seek out, and ponder—

I am afraid of knowing, and *not* knowing,
but I am more afraid
of living without this little compass,
this pocketful of faith
that guides me when I cannot see
what lies before me

even when i'm sleepwalking

Some days come and go
and I wonder if I even thought
about anything at all—
Sometimes I wonder
if I'm sleepwalking
throughout my entire existence—
I wonder if I've ever truly
been present for a moment

But other days,
I know I'm alive—
My spirit is on fire
and I feel it kindling
more fervently than ever

My mind is a whirlwind of thoughts
and if I don't write them down,
they'll hold me hostage—
so I let them loose,
getting rid of them
in every way I know how—
pressing them into paper—
and onto keyboards
of computers and typewriters—

I scribble them on any surface I can find:
receipts, napkins, notebooks, walls,
the back of my own hands, even—

These are my favorite days—
the days I'm so ensnared by living
that I have to capture it
The days the sunsets are more than brilliant
and the people, too—
The days I spend arranging bouquets of words
with my muse being *all of creation*

Heartache and all,
I'm thankful to be alive—
even on days I'm sleepwalking

patience and purity

My home is in the mountains,
but not on a plot of land.
It's *two people* who have always held
my heart inside their hands.

My dad embodies Patience,
and my mom, Purity.
Together, they are both examples
of who I strive to be.

There's a house beside a pond,
there's a porch made with Patient hands.
There are three small rooms down a hall
where Purity tucked us each in bed.

There's a living room for time well-spent,
there's a room for Purity to quilt.
There's a long, gravel driveway
near a barn where Patience works and builds.

There's a fenced-in yard for doggies,
there are woods for all of us to explore.
There's a tall, muddy embankment
beside a concrete, basketball court.

There is Patience's sense of humor,
There is Purity's contagious laugh.
But there is discipline when needed
to keep us on a steady path.

Mom and Dad, I love you.
Thank you for all the love you've shown.
Thank you for your wisdom;
it is because of *you* I've grown.

My spirit has always loved to wander,
my feet have always loved to roam—
but no matter where I choose to be,
my heart is always home.

t h i s   m o m e n t

Sit a while with me.
Wherever you are reading this from,
a bed, a balcony, a bench, a backseat;
whatever you are doing, it doesn't matter.
All that matters is that you are
exclusively and entirely *you*.
Sit here for a second and think about
how you are the only one present for this very moment;
How no one else is breathing your air—
How your sky isn't the same shade of blue
as someone else's—
How the world looks a little different for everyone—
How you are the *only one* inhabiting the territory
of your wild and unfeigned thoughts

How spectacular it is to be purely *you*—
How magnificent it is to live in a world
where there are no replicates—
There will always be some wondrous thing
that makes you unlike anyone else.

I think it is easy to slip into feeling alone;
but even though we are living this moment separately,
we are in it together.
I wrote these words already, but I was thinking of *you*
and of this moment we are both in
from our dwelling places across the world—
and I hope these words extend out to you
like a warm hug, a gentle embrace reminding you
that *you are not alone.*

There will always be
some wondrous thing
that makes you
unlike anyone else.

two directions

There are two places we can choose to dwell;
what lies ahead or *what lies behind.*
I've found it easiest to let the past
take throne inside my mind.
I carry so much luggage
from the places that I've been,
that making room for more
is a hard task to begin.
One by one, I'll dump the bags;
sort them through and through.
I'll carry what's good with me,
and the bad, I'll toss askew.
There are two places we can choose to dwell,
but I'm looking forward every day.
The burdens that once plagued me
are no longer in my way.
I look behind from time to time,
but my focus is on *today.*
I am living in the present;
in the past, I'll never stay.

The ~~burden~~ burdens that once plagued me are no longer in my way.

There's two places we can choose to dwell;
What's ahead or what's behind
I've found its easiest to let
The past take ~~the~~ throne inside my mind
I carry so much luggage from the places tha~~t~~
~~proven~~
...ting room to make more space, is a har~~d~~
...is proving difficult to begin [task t...]
One by one, I'll dump the bags,
sort them through and through,

this dandelion-wish life

Life is made up of highs and lows. Throughout the day, we constantly scroll through "highlights" and forget that everyone has their "lowlights," too. It is important to remember that beneath our aesthetics and angles, we are all human. We are all united through our experiences; knowing that no matter who we are or where we are from, we are all a part of humanity. We are all maneuvering through these highs and lows together.

We all have one chance at this dandelion-wish life. If we don't pay attention, in a gust, it will be over. I don't want to waste mine wishing on someone else's story. I want my own story; lowlights and all. I want to die knowing I have lived my life and not someone else's.

We all have one chance
at this dandelion-wish life.

If we don't pay attention,
in a gust, it will be over.

melodies and stories

I woke up this morning
and the only plan I wanted to make
for my day was dancing,
and the only thing I wanted to be was music—
each of my footsteps a beat
in this glorious soundtrack of life

And if I was brave enough to pretend that
I didn't care what people thought,
I would run out my front door,
barefooted and doing handsprings,
and somersaulting down the streets
and up the sidewalks,
and screaming to the neighbors,

Something about songs
and how we are all dancing melodies—
Something about books
and how we are all walking stories—
Something about the earth
and how it's our memoir—
and our feet, the pens!
Our voices, too!
Everything we are and do!

We are all writing,
grafting our stories
into the binding of the universe,

and I woke up this morning
terrified of not living a story worth telling
and not telling a story worth living—

I don't want to live my life without commas,
or semicolons, or a few plot twists—
and I don't want to reach the end of my story
and wonder what it was about.

I want to dog-ear every page
in this chapter of life we are sharing.
And right now?
I'm going to start by dancing.

r e c i p e   f o r   l i v i n g

Yesterday came and left so quickly
I wonder if I was even there for it at all
This morning I woke
and realized
I forgot to relish in it—
forgot to marinate in its sunlight—
savor the sound
of the songbirds' final cries of jubilee
before winter feeds their silence

What did I do yesterday?—
except fill it with empty conversations,
leaving it malnourished
and in want of something real

Sometimes I think that I'm immortal—
like tomorrow will always be here for me
But *today is fleeting,*
so I will sift it of all its hatred
and knead out any bitterness
I will glaze it with love,
garnish it with intentionality,
sprinkle it with sweetness and benevolence
I will rise with each day
and preserve it carefully—
I won't allow it
to stale or fester with mold

This is my recipe for living—
it is not meant to be stored in a box
or exchanged in hushed whispers—
It is meant to be echoed from the mountaintops
for the whole world to hear:

Today is meant for us to partake in

RECIPE FOR LIVING

Main ingredient: Today

1. Sift it of all its hatred
2. Knead out any bitterness
3. Glaze it with love
4. Garnish it with intentionality
5. Sprinkle it with sweetness and benevolence
6. Rise with each day and preserve it carefully
7. Share with everyone!

Use this recipe every day for not just a fulfilling
day, but a fulfilling life! And always remember,
today is meant for us to partake in. :)

Dear Reader,

I used to wish my heart had training wheels. I used to want to keep my heart in perfect condition. But if it didn't have any scars, would I have even used it? Would I truly know the meaning of living if I hadn't known the meaning of losing? I don't think I would. Looking back, I can see that I would have done some things differently. I have made plenty of mistakes along this rugged ride. But this basket of mistakes has taught me a lot about how to live my life. I still have an infinite amount to learn. Now, off to some more lessons. Maybe I'll see you there.

All my love,

Ellen

OPEN CAMERA APP
AND SCAN FOR A
SURPRISE :)

my dad teaching me
to ride my bicycle
in my grandparents' driveway

thank you dad,
for being a teacher, a giver,
and just for being my dad.
i'm so proud to be your daughter.
i love you so much.

Printed in Great Britain
by Amazon

24851804R00187